RIVERBANK

RIVERBANK

A Tragic-comedy
Or
The Upside Of Memory Loss

A Play In Two Acts

By

MARILYN MAPLE PH.D.

Printed in the United States of America.

ISBN: 978-1-4269-3973-0 (sc)
ISBN: 978-1-4269-3974-7 (e)

Trafford rev. 02/17/2011

 www.trafford.com

North America & International
toll-free: 1 888 232 4444 (USA & Canada)
phone: 250 383 6864 ✦ fax: 812 355 4082

This Play is dedicated to:

Peg Foust, M.A.,
Judith Williams, Ph.D.,
Edmund Ackell, M.D., D.M.D.,
And Edward Albee
For their encouragement and inspiration.

TABLE OF CONTENTS

ACT I

ACT II

CAST OF CHARACTERS

Jenny Kraus:
90 year old mother of Charlie Kraus, suffering from senile dementia, comes to live with his family – wife and five children, all of whom she doesn't remember.

Charlie Kraus:
Father and husband, seventy, Professor of Chemistry at a local university. Charlie once worked for a refinery in New Jersey but opted to teach at a university because it better suited his ivory tower preferred lifestyle.

Kate Kraus:
Kate is 58, wife of Charlie and mother of the five Kraus children. Kate is a hedonist, much more worldly wise than Charlie, She has led a rather varied existence but sacrificed all to achieve her childhood dream as an only child – to have a home and family.

Austin Kraus:
Austin is twenty-eight, the oldest child. He is a drug dealer. He has always resented not being an only child and therefore spends most of his time maintaining his status by being a bully.

Lissa Kraus:
Is twenty-seven, She and Austin are "Irish Twins" being born just one year apart. She is gay, a teacher of deaf, blind, and other disabled children in California and has a significant other.

Becky Kraus:
Is twenty-five, and works in a child care center. She is slightly promiscuous because her only goal in life is to get married and have a family. As a middle child she craves the love and attention that her mother receives.

Byron Kraus:
Is twenty-three, very bright, depressed, and a pacifist. He has a college degree but works in the library. He is philosophic but lacks direction and incentive. He too is a middle child but has given up on getting attention.

Casey Kraus:
Casey is the youngest child, twenty. He is a part-time student and has a job as a cook at a local restaurant. As the youngest child he is loved by all with the possible exception of Austin.

Eric:
Eric is Casey's friend who has been kicked out of his own house by his father.

TIME: Afternoon- 1982 - Over a two month period.

SETTING: Living room in complete disarray with papers, empty soda and beer cans, paper plates, etc., scattered everywhere. Every piece of furniture (couch, overstuffed chair and rocking chair) has some debris on it and the floor is also littered. The rocking chair is located on the left side of the room facing the hall door. A radio is on, very low, to a rock station. The kitchen is behind the living room and from the living room one can see dishes piled high in the sink, a refrigerator, a stove with a large soup pot on it, and general clutter. A kitchen counter extends into the living room area as a quasi room divider and bar. Atop the counter is a toaster, can opener, telephone books, and junk. A wall phone is located just above the bar and also a bulletin board with all kinds of numbers and pictures on the board. Under the bar there is at least one bottle of scotch and glasses.

Scene opens with nothing but a pinpoint light on the rocking chair which is on the left side of the stage then slowly lights are brought up to reveal Kate. Once Kate is established in light, another pinpoint light shows Charlie talking to her by phone. Lights are up full when Casey and Eric enter.

ACT I

Scene I

KATE

(Puffing on a cigarette and talking on phone with a
long extension cord to CHARLIE, her husband.)
Who's been taking care of her?

CHARLIE

Her neighbor. But she's getting too old to handle her.

KATE

How about nursing homes?

CHARLIE

Kate, even if we get a good price for the house, we can't afford a nursing
home. It costs three, four, five thousand a month.

KATE

You're right. We can't afford that.

CHARLIE

Our only option is to bring her home with me. If
(KATE moves items on the bar around aimlessly... drops
ashes on floor, moves toaster and several cockroaches
run out. She starts hitting at them.)
I'm lucky I can get a couple of tickets out of here today and be home
tomorrow at the latest. What in the hell are you doing?

KATE

What?

> (Putting cigarette in mouth and slapping another cockroach.)

What do you mean, what am I doing? I'm killing Goddam cockroaches, that's what I'm doing.

KATE

> (Listening)

I suppose you have to bring her here, but I'm not too sure she can take it. How is she going to handle a house full of kids? How is she going to handle the craziness of this place?

(ENTER CASEY with friend ERIC.)

CASEY carries basketball under arm. They head for the refrigerator to get a beer. KATE notices them and pulls a bottle of scotch out from under the bar. She pours herself a hefty slug of scotch into a Styrofoam sipper cup holding the phone with one hand and with the cigarette held in her mouth.)

CHARLIE

She'll handle it.

KATE

Yeah, well, it's your mother but this place could drive her crazy. I mean.

> (Quietly she calls to CASEY.)

Casey. Casey.

> (She tries to reach the sink but the extension cord isn't long enough and then starts motioning to CASEY - catches his eye and mouths WATER.)

KATE

You're really all wrapped up in this aren't you?

2

(CASEY comes over picks up his Mother's sipper, pours in some water from the tap and returns the sipper to her.)

CASEY

(In a low voice.)
You're gonna turn into an old drunk, Kate.

KATE

(Laughs silently and pushes him aside.)
Charlie, Charlie... listen to me.
                    (She turns her back away from boys toward audience and the conversation continues between KATE and CHARLIE silently.)

ERIC

That your Ma?

CASEY

Yeah, name's Kate.

ERIC

You call her Kate? Not Mom?

(CASEY and ERIC move into living room where they commence picking up papers, while they make the move toward the living room.)

CASEY

Kate... Mom. She comes to anything.

(CASEY seats himself on the couch after cleaning off an area. ERIC stands. The boys continue to talk in low voices—toss ball back and forth.)

ERIC

Does she always drink out of one of those?

CASEY

Yeah. I think it's because she figures she doesn't have to fill it up that often, and nobody can see what she's drinking or how much.

ERIC

Pretty smart huh?
(Beat)
My old man drinks.

CASEY

Kate's a mellow drinker.

ERIC

I wish he was.
(Beat)
I gotta get a job. I can't go home again. I gotta get some income so I can get an apartment.

CASEY

I just gotta promotion... Hey! I got promoted from dishwasher to short-order cook where I work. So we gotta dishwasher job open. It's not bad. Upward mobility and all that shit ... ya want it I'll put a good word in for ya?

ERIC

I want it.
(They talk together.)

CHARLIE

Stop worrying about how she'll take to us. At this point she doesn't remember or relate to anything. She doesn't even remember me. (Pause) But, I'll change that. I know I can help her regain some sense of reality.

KATE

You're a good one for that (sarcastically) ... well, I really don't care about her head. That's your problem. What I want to know is, how's her body?

CHARLIE

What do you mean?

KATE

What do you mean, what do I mean? I mean, does she wet her pants?

CHARLIE

No more than you do.

KATE

Oh, that's cute! Okay, Charlie, does she get around. Does she walk? What can I expect from a 90 year old mother-in-law that I haven't seen in over 10 years?

> (KATE turns her back from audience lowers voice and continues conversation.
> ERIC starts to sit in the rocking chair.)

CASEY

That's my brother's rocking chair.

ERIC:

Yeah?

> (Changes his mind and sits on the other chair.)

CASEY

Yeah, Austin doesn't like anyone to sit in his rocking chair.

ERIC

Not even Goldilocks?

(Settles himself more comfortably in the over-stuffed chair.)

CASEY

All of us are rockers, except my sister Lissa. Each kid has a rocking chair, it's just that Austin is the oldest and he gets to have his in the living room. (Beat) We even body rock when we get up tight, except Lissa. (Laughs) I guess that's because Austin used to rock us when we were kids ... all except Lissa. They were both too young for him to rock her, just a year apart.

ERIC

How big is your family?

CASEY

Five kids. Mom had five in seven years.

ERIC

Wow! And Austin is your big brother?

CASEY

(With mouth full.)
Yeah, he's the oldest, 28. I'm 20 and then there's Byron, you've met him, he's 23.

ERIC
Yeah, just to say "hello". What's Austin do?

CASEY

Anyone and anything he can.
(As an afterthought he adds:)
He's a semi dealer-farmer- courier. Sells more than he grows though.

ERIC

Drugs?

CASEY

Yeah, and grass.

ERIC

You separate the two?

CASEY

I guess I do. I don't think grass can fuck up your brain like hard drugs.

ERIC
Your parents know?

CASEY

Yeah. You have to understand them. They figure everyone's of age, 'cept me and I'm pretty self-reliant. They have always brought us up to make our own choices and live with the consequences.
ERIC
Man! That's easy living. My old man does drugs, but if he ever caught me, I'd be dead.

CASEY

Well I guess Charlie and Kate are what they call permissive, but they always wanted us to grow up as real individuals.
(Pause)
And we did.

(ENTER BECKY)
BECKY

Hi. Who are you?

ERIC

I'm Eric.
BECKY

I'm Becky.   Mom's on the phone?

CASEY

That's an intelligent observation. By the way, Eric is going to be moving in with me for a while.

BECKY

Oh good.
(Flops on couch seductively.)

CASEY

Yeah, I've been trying to explain the family to him.

BECKY

(Laughs) Oh, I'd like to hear that.

CASEY

Well, if you're so smart, tell him how come Kate and Charlie are so permissive.

BECKY

Well, for Dad, I think he figures we're Kate's responsibility. Mom, she's different. She told me her philosophy about raising children when I first started working at the nursery school. There was a book she read that said something about parents are the bows that shoot the arrows in the air.

CASEY

So we're the arrows!

BECKY
(Trying to remember.)
It was a little book called…
(Remembering)
"The Prophet". It said something about once the arrows are in the air they follow their own destiny.

CASEY

They sure shot a quiver full.

ERIC

Yeah. Five of you. You told me about four, who's number five?

CASEY

(Laughs)
That's Lissa. You don't have to worry about her. She's out in California. She teaches deaf and blind kids.

BECKY

Yeah, She's really different.

CASEY

(Shooting BECKY a look.)
We're all different.

BECKY

It's a good family. I want a family just like it.

CASEY

It's a circus!
(KATE turns around hangs up phone with a quiet slam. Pinpoint light out on CHARLIE.)

KATE

Well, here we go!

CASEY

That was Dad?

KATE

Yes... and guess what?

CASEY

Ma, I'm not a mind reader.

KATE

(Ignoring his comment.)

He's bringing your Grandmother down here to live with us... (In wonderment) your 90 year-old Grandmother, Jenny Kraus.

CASEY

90! Are you sure she's 90?

BECKY

God, I didn't know she was that old.

KATE

You probably don't remember her. She used to hand out Christmas gifts to all of you, but she could never remember your names so everyone had to switch gifts after she left. She lived in her own world then, can you imagine what she's like now?

CASEY

Dad lives in his own world. So what's new? (Beat) So, how did this come about?

KATE

The neighbor who has been kind of taking care of her called and said that she was worse and that she couldn't cope with her anymore. So Charlie went up to New Jersey. I guess he checked into nursing homes, but they were too expensive. Even if he got a good price for the house, it was out of our range.

CASEY

So, we're the nursing home. This should be interesting.

KATE

It certainly should. (Beat) Hi. Who are you?

ERIC

I'm Eric, Casey's friend.

KATE

Oh, of course, it's nice to meet you finally, Eric.
(KATE shakes his hand.)
(Beat)
You know she never came to our wedding because my mother insisted
we have it in the Catholic Church and Jenny, like your Dad, was a
Christian Scientist

(KATE starts to exit room through hall door. BECKY
goes to get a beer from the refrigerator.)

CASEY

Hey Ma, how come I don't remember her?

KATE

(Thoughtfully)
Your Grandmother? You were so young. We used to visit her about
three or four times a year. Then we moved down here and offered to
pay her way down, because you kids didn't want to go up there, and
taking all of you in the car on any trip was just a disaster. Well, she
never wanted to travel. So we haven't seen her. Oh your Dad has. He
went up once a year- well, not in the last few years... he's been busy.

CASEY

When is Dad coming back from New Jersey?

KATE

(Stops her exit.)
Who knows? Tomorrow, or the next day.

ERIC

Mrs. Kraus?

KATE

Kate

ERIC

Kate. With Casey's Grandmother coming maybe I shouldn't stay over here.

(BECKY enters and sits on couch.)

CASEY

Yeah, Ma. I forgot to tell you. I invited Eric to move in with his guitar. He can stay in my room. He's just going to hang out here for a while I mean. His old man kicked him out. Okay?

KATE

It's okay with me. What's one more.
(Beat)
Oh. BEDS. Let's see, I'll have to put Jenny in your room Becky, and I'll move Byron in with Austin and you and Eric can move into Byron's room.

BECKY

Mom, you don't have to worry about me. I've been hanging out with this guy and he really wants me to move in, so I'll just move my stuff and nobody has to move around. Besides, I don't think Byron would really like moving in with Austin.

KATE

You're probably right. Okay then, Eric, just move your stuff into Casey's room. (Beat) By the way, isn't your Dad a musician?

ERIC

Yeah. He's not home too much, but when he comes home all hell breaks loose.

KATE

That's gotta be tough… on your mother too.

ERIC

It is, that's why I need to get out, get a job and an apartment so she'll have some place to go.

KATE

She must be proud of you. Do you have any brothers or sisters?

ERIC

I had a brother, but he died in an accident. I was too young to remember, but... I think my Dad figures the wrong one died.

BECKY

That's horrible!

KATE

Oh, no Eric, he couldn't possibly!

ERIC

Well, I wish you were right.

KATE

Are you a musician like your Dad?

ERIC

I play the guitar and I write some music but, I'm not good like he is.

KATE

Maybe someday you'll be better than he is. Think about it.

ERIC

Sometimes I do... but I don't think he'd like that. Besides, we don't like the same kind of music. I write songs, like protest songs against violence, or harming the environment... that kind of stuff.

KATE

Oh, well, you and Byron will get along well. Do you know Byron?

ERIC

I think I met him at a kind of jam session once. He's plays the guitar too, doesn't he?

KATE

Yes, but not as well as Casey and I'm sure, not as well as you. Byron should be home pretty soon. You'll come to know all of us soon enough. You just stay here as long as you need to get on your feet.

CASEY

I'm pretty sure I can get him a job.

ERIC

I'll pay my way, you know, rent and stuff.

KATE

Don't sweat it, if you can put up with this family… you'll be paying your dues.

(EXIT KATE)

ERIC

Well, with me and your grandmother coming, looks like the family's gettin' bigger.

CASEY

(Pre-occupied)

Yeah, Hey Becky, so you gotta new John you can go live with.

(Aside to Eric.)

You gotta know, Becky only goes with guys named John, that's so she doesn't get them mixed up.

BECKY

What's the matter Casey, jealous? I don't see you bringing any girls home.

CASEY

A lot of girls like me. I just don't talk about it.

ERIC

I've seen some of them; they're pretty cool.

CASEY

Don't tell her. (Beat) Hey, what's this current John like?

BECKY

None of your Goddam business.

(Flouncing off stage in direction of Kate.)

Hey Mom, whatever happened to that book… you know "The Prophet"?

KATE
(From somewhere in the house.)
I don't know, you'll have to look for it. Better still, ask Charlie when he gets home.

CASEY
(Laughing)
Good old Becky, whenever we have to play musical beds, it's always Becky who gets to move out cause she can always find a guy to move in with.

ERIC

That's okay with your Mom?

CASEY

I guess so
(Considers question, then)
Yeah. I guess it's just the arrow following its course in destiny.

(ENTER BYRON who has overheard the last comment.)

Well, well, look who's home... you're overdue from the library. Bet you just did volumes of work today.

BYRON
Yeah, all day long stacking books.
(Plops down on couch - looks at Eric.)
Hey, didn't we meet at some concert to save the Suwannee River?

ERIC
Yeah, that's where it was. I was trying to remember.

BYRON
Man, you play a mean guitar. I wish I could play that well.

CASEY
Well, maybe he can give you lessons. Eric's staying here for a while.

BYRON
Hey that's great! Eric. That's your name? Is your dad--

CASEY
(Interrupting)
Yeah ... yeah, but right now he'd just as soon forget about his dad. That's why he's staying here.

BYRON
Oh, okay.
(Pause)
Sometimes I have trouble with my dad too.

CASEY
What do you mean?

(ENTER AUSTIN, unseen.)

BYRON

Just that everybody says I'm like Dad and I don't want to be like Dad. I wanna be like me.

(AUSTIN seats himself in his rocking chair.)

AUSTIN

What do you mean? You'd be lucky to be like Father.

CASEY

Ahhh, this is Austin. Austin this is Eric. Eric is gonna be staying in my room for a while. Oh, and by the way, our Charlie is bringing our 90 year-old Grandmother to stay with us too. So you might have to clean up your act.

ERIC

(A little fearfully.)

Nice meeting you, Austin. (Beat) Hey Byron, I'm going back to Casey's room. Bring your guitar back and we'll jam.

(EXIT ERIC)

BYRON

Nice guy! It'll be fun having him here.

AUSTIN

Shit! (Rocking)

CASEY

Hey, you and Byron just missed rooming together, you can thank Becky for having a new John to move in with … wouldn't that have been sweet?

(BYRON casts a look of relief at AUSTIN as he EXITS.)

AUSTIN

Shit!

(Rocks faster.)

CASEY

(Laughing)

Another intelligent reaction! As the arrows scatter in the air, following their destinies, to who knows where, you sit in your rocking chair.

(EXIT CASEY. AUSTIN sits and rocks.)

(Lights come down to pinpoint light on chair.)

(Lights dim and then go to black.)

ACT I

<u>Scene II</u>

(At Rise: One Day later. Afternoon.
Setting: Living Room has been cleaned up. The rocking chair which had been designated as AUSTIN'S has been moved to the right side of the room near the hall exit... but facing audience. To further emphasize the chair, there is pinpoint lighting over the chair...to set it apart from the other furniture.   CHARLIE is helping JENNY through the door and seating her in the rocking chair. At this point the only lighting on the stage is the pinpoint light on the chair and low fill light... it is low so that the rest of the family who are standing in the kitchen area are silhouetted... and as the family is introduced to JENNY the lights begin to get brighter and brighter with each introduction until the last person when lights are up full.)

JENNY
(In a thin weak voice.)
Thank you very much. You're a very nice gentleman.

CHARLIE
Now, Mother, you know you're my mother and I'm your son, Charles, and this is my house - but now it's your new home.
(He motions to KATE.)

Now, you have to meet the family.

You knew all of them years ago, but you haven't seen them in quite some time. This is Kate, my wife.

KATE

Hi, Jenny, remember me?

JENNY
(Extends hand.)

Oh yes.
(False certainty in her voice.)

I … I think so.

(AUSTIN steps forward.)

CHARLIE

Mother, this is your oldest grandson, Austin.

AUSTIN

Hello, Grandmother, Father told us all about you and that's my rocking chair you're sitting in...
(KATE smacks him on the rear end.) (Pause)

you'll like it, it's the best rocking chair in the house.

JENNY

Thank you.
(BYRON steps forward.)

BYRON

Hi, I'm Byron… what do you want us to call you?

JENNY
(Little girl—like.)

My name is Jenny.

BYRON

Okay, Jenny, and this is Becky.

BECKY

Hi Jenny.
> (She speaks like she speaks to children in the daycare center.)

Would you like some tea or a cup of coffee or something?

JENNY

Oh, that would be nice.

BECKY

Tea?
> (BECKY is already on her way to kitchen.)

JENNY

Yes, thank you.

CASEY

Hi Jenny, I'm Casey.

JENNY

Oh,
> (Extending hand.)

I'm pleased to meet you.

> (CASEY and AUSTIN go over to sit on couch. CASEY reaches around behind the couch and finds the basketball and starts to play with it, BYRON sits on floor near couch.)

CHARLIE

Well, that's the family except for Lissa, she's out in California.

JENNY

Thank you all very much. You are all very nice.
> (Pauses. looks around.)

This is a lovely hotel. I'm not too sure I can afford it.
> (Pauses as she senses a need.)

Do you have a public bathroom? Ohhhh.

KATE

Oh, yes, let me help you. It's right down this hall.
> (JENNY shuffles along with KATE holding her from behind.)

> (KATE casts a questioning look at CHARLIE over her shoulder. CHARLIE catches the look, turns his back and lights a cigar and walks out of the room.)

> (CHARLIE EXITS back of stage.)

> (AUSTIN gets up off couch, goes over to rocking chair and stares at it… sets it to rocking with his hand…and then goes over and sits in the overstuffed chair.)

> (CASEY puts ball down and gets up and goes to the kitchen where BECKY is standing with a teapot in hand.)

> (CASEY gets a beer from the refrigerator.)

AUSTIN

> (Yells as he rocks the rocker.)

Shit! Get me one. (Pause)
Bring some bourbon too!

CASEY

How 'bout you, Byron?

BYRON

No, I don't think so.
> (Moving into a lotus position and rocking.)

AUSTIN
> (Body rocking in over stuffed chair.)

Christ, she's out of her head!

CASEY

Yeah.

(Sensing an undercurrent in Austin's remark.)

Yeah.

(Handing the beer and bourbon bottle to AUSTIN and pausing to sip his own. With sarcasm.)

Afraid it runs in the family?

AUSTIN

Shit! I'll take you on any day.

(Taking a sip of bourbon and a sip of beer.)

CASEY

Yeah, Mr. Big Shot. All you do is think about yourself. You ought to think about Mom. She's gonna bear the brunt of this. You and your fucking chair and ego.

BYRON

Poor Mom!

CASEY

Poor Mom!

(CASEY walks over and leans on bar.)

BYRON

As if she doesn't have enough work.

AUSTIN

She'll handle it. Speaking of work, Mom said to tell you that your parrot's in the back room picking the drapes off the curtain rods. Oh, and also, Leonardo, your sweet little boa constrictor has let himself out of the cage again and is somewhere in the house.

BYRON

Okay. Okay. Okay. He's probably curled up some place. I just fed him, actually I overfed him.   He'll be okay for weeks.

CASEY

Crap, is that all you guys think about? Parrots and boas. Think about that old lady. She's our grandmother. Dad's mother. Part of her is part of us and she's so old…and so… frail... so out of it.

> (CASEY puts head down on bar. Tears start to come and he tries to hide them by turning away. BECKY ENTERS from the kitchen, puts tea down and tries to hug him and he pulls away from her.)

God! She's so old… and she's gonna die… and she's gonna die right here!

> (There is a poignant pause from the whole group.)

AUSTIN

Everybody dies… especially here.

BYRON

Casey's not as jaded as the rest of us. He's right. She's gonna die here. If you were gonna die, would you choose to die in a place like this?

> (BECKY goes back to kitchen, then comes back in to join the group.)

BECKY

Boy, she's in bad shape! (Pause) Times like this, I wish I was in California with Lissa.

BYRON

> (Almost a commentary to himself.)

She doesn't even know Dad.

CASEY

That bothers him too... you can tell.

AUSTIN

Well, wouldn't it bother you if your own mother didn't know you?
(Group silence. Digesting the situation.)

BECKY

(With a nervous laugh.)
You know, Dad's a lot like her. I mean, you know, how he forgets things... calls me Lissa sometimes.

CASEY

(Laughing)
Yeah, remember the time Dad went out to play tennis. He had his sweat suit on. He got too hot, and took off the top. Then he got hotter and took the bottoms off. He'd forgotten to put his underwear on,
(Laughs)
standin' there naked as a Jay bird.

BYRON

Are you saying it runs in the family?

AUSTIN

(To self)
I forget everything... forget where I put things... I'm paranoid as a cat- oh fuck!
(Takes another drink.)

BYRON

If you'd cut out the drugs.

AUSTIN

If you'd shut your Goddam mouth.

CASEY

Leave him alone, if he keeps it up he'll ... lose his mind by the time he's 35. All the gray matter will have turned chartreuse.

BYRON

Bile green.

AUSTIN

SHUT-UP.

BECKY

Oh, come on. Leave him alone.
> (She goes over and rubs AUSTIN'S shoulders.)

I think I'm glad I'm the one that has to move out.

BYRON

Why?

BECKY

I don't think I could take it.

CASEY

Take what. All we have is a little 90 year-old lady who has come to live with us and everyone thinks it's some big deal.

BECKY

You look at her and you realize that everyone has to die sometime, and I've thought about death so often that I really don't need to have it confronting me every day.

BYRON

Why do you think of death so much?

BECKY

Oh, I don't know. Everything goes so wrong for me. You guys laugh at me whenever I go to live with some new guy but, I want a home and kids so badly and sometimes I think. I'll never have them.

AUSTIN
You want a home and kids after living in this family, God!

CASEY
(Walking around.)
Hey, this family is okay.

BYRON
(In a thoughtful mood.)
I guess I think about death too, but I think more about not killing other things than killing myself,   (Pause)
but sometimes I think about that too.

(Group silence)

You know, in Zen... they say a prayer asking forgiveness for the bugs they step on during the day.

CASEY
Forget the bugs! What we have here is an old, tired body, waiting to die and be buried.

BYRON
The answer to a bug's prayer.

CASEY
Christ, you're morbid.

(BECKY goes back into kitchen to get the teapot and puts it on the table near the rocking chair, then sits down on couch.
AUSTIN is rolling a reefer. He lights it.)

BYRON
It's depressing.

CASEY

Everything is depressing to you. Life's depressing. Death is depressing. What the hell isn't depressing.

AUSTIN

Anyone for a toke?

CASEY

Naw.

BYRON

Pass.

BECKY

I'll take one.

(Inhales slowly. and hands it back to AUSTIN. Upon hearing his mother's voice, AUSTIN EXITS taking the brief case with him.)

(KATE ENTERS bringing JENNY in and seats her in the chair. She talks while she seats her. She takes off JENNY's jacket, then takes off her sweater, only to find another sweater underneath and she takes that off too. Then begins to pick up the debris in the room, almost obsessively.)

KATE

Well, Jenny's seen most of the house now, haven't you?

JENNY

I guess so.

(She looks at CASEY and BYRON.)

It's very nice here but I'm going to have to go home soon. Do you boys know how far I am away from my home? I'll need to get started soon.

BYRON
(Interrupts)
You're about 1500 miles from home, Jenny.

JENNY
(Laughs)
Oh, you're just kidding me.

BYRON
No, Jenny, you're in Florida now - not New Jersey.

JENNY
But I live in New Jersey.

(KATE has stopped picking up things and has dropped herself into the big over- stuffed chair and has found some mail between the arm and the pillow and sets about reading it. BECKY who has been observing this, gets up from the couch and goes over to refill the cup of tea.
BECKY kneels down by the chair and speaks to JENNY as if she were a child. JENNY takes the cup and looks at BECKY in a questioning way.)

BECKY
You know Jenny, I'm your namesake.
(BECKY sees the blank look.)
My name is Jenny Rebecca.

JENNY
I'm a registered nurse, you know.

BECKY
Oh really? I'm your granddaughter, you know.

JENNY

Oh no.

(In total disbelief.)
I don't have grandchildren. I'm too young.

BECKY

(Patting JENNY's hand.)
How old do you think you are, Jenny?

JENNY

Oh, let's see, I must be somewhere in my thirties by now.

(BECKY looks over at her mother who returns the look. There is a pause then, KATE shakes her head.)

KATE

Me too, Jenny. Life keeps playing these terrible hoaxes on us, doesn't it? Want some hot soup Jenny?
(KATE EXITS to get some soup.
BECKY stands up and pats JENNY on the head and slowly EXITS via the same hall.)

CASEY

(Stands up awkwardly.)
See ya later, Grand ...Jenny.

(ENTER ERIC)
ERIC

Hey, I got the job! I start tomorrow. Man, am I happy!
(He spots JENNY.)
Oh, I'm sorry for interrupting.

CASEY

Oh,

(Guiding ERIC over to JENNY.)
meet my grandmother, this is my friend Eric, he lives here too.

ERIC

How do you do, ma'am.

> (Looks at CASEY with confusion and then shakes JENNY's hand.)

JENNY

> (With a sweet smile.)

My name is Jenny.

ERIC

Very nice to meet you, Jenny.

CASEY

We'll see you at dinner Jenny.

> (To ERIC)

Come on.

ERIC

I gotta get some stuff out of my car. I'll just be a minute.

> (EXIT CASEY and ERIC)

BYRON

> (Getting up from the floor.)

Yeah, we'll see you at dinner.

> (EXIT BYRON. ENTER KATE with soup.)

KATE

Well, Jenny, I guess we're going to get to know each other for the first time, really.

> (She tries to hand the bowl to JENNY who doesn't take it, then she begins to feed her. KATE opens her mouth and JENNY opens hers. KATE shoves the soup in. After two mouthfuls JENNY pushes the bowl away.)

That's it? That's all you want? Another cooking rejection slip! Okay, I guess all you want is a little peace...and God knows, this is the last place to come for peace.

(JENNY nods as if tired.)

(ENTER ERIC unnoticed he sees KATE EXIT and quietly listens . Lights have been dimming as each person has EXITED. Now there is just a pinpoint light on JENNY as JENNY sings.)

JENNY
(Rocks and hums quietly in her old frail voice.)

We are going down the valley one by one

With our faces toward the setting sun

One by one the cares of life forever pass

And we shall stand upon the riverbank at last.

Light dims to black.

ACT I

Scene III

(At Rise: Same day, later that evening.
Setting: Living Room. CHARLIE is reading a book when KATE enters.)

KATE

Well, I got four layers of clothes off her finally. Jenny's in bed and I think she'll sleep. Want a drink?
(Walking to the kitchen area.)

CHARLIE

I have my bourbon.

KATE

Boy we're almost out of scotch. I've gotta get some tomorrow.
(She wanders back to CHARLIE.)
Charlie, we have to talk about your mother.
(Pause - she walks around.)
Charlie, we have to talk.
(Pause)
Charlie, what are you reading?

CHARLIE

Ah, "The Origin of Consciousness in the Breakdown of the Bicameral Mind".
(He takes a drink.)

KATE

Sounds fascinating!
(Sarcastically)
Charlie, now that I have your attention. We have to talk.

CHARLIE

About what? My mother?

KATE

Look, I don't mind her coming here. I don't mind taking care of her because I figure, eventually we'll have my mother here so I can't complain. My mother still has her mind and her sharp tongue so your mother is easier. But...

CHARLIE

(Interrupts)
My mother will be just fine. Tomorrow is Sunday and I will take her to the Christian Science Church. She'll feel better among those ideas that are familiar to her. Also, I plan to kind of find out where her mind is, you know, what year she thinks this is and then I'll gradually bring her forward, even if I have to regress myself. She'll be okay.

KATE

Charlie, she's not going to be okay. Oh God, how can you as a scientist say she's going to be okay? By the way, how can she be a nurse and a Christian Scientist?

CHARLIE

I'm a scientist and a Christian Scientist, even though I'm no longer a member of the church. As to my mother, well, she just had greater powers of healing because she could practice nursing and enhance it with Christian Science.

KATE

Charlie, get real, she has Alzheimer's or some kind of senile dementia.

CHARLIE

Kate, she has not been diagnosed with that.

KATE

Of course not, she's never been to a doctor.

CHARLIE

(Continuing his thought.)

That's where the conflict arises. Scientists like doctors have to label everything. Christian Science doesn't. It allows for more individualistic concepts about the etiology of disease or aberration.

KATE

Charlie, I don't want to hear.

CHARLIE

A scientist found something and named it for himself "Alzheimer's" and suppose other scientists find other forms of the same disease do they name that after themselves. The smart thing to do would be label a disease as x and then as discoveries are made, you just add exponents, x squared, x to the third power and x to the fourth power.

KATE

(Interrupts)

Charlie, I am going to X you right out of my life. This is now, it's not hypothetical. This is reality. Your mother had four layers of clothes on her today. I don't know when she last had a bath and you are not taking her to church tomorrow. I am giving her a bath. Do you understand. All your far flung plans to give her back her mind are out until next Sunday. Tomorrow she cleans her body.

CHARLIE

If you knew what you were going to do, why did you bother asking me in the first place?

KATE

I suppose because I figured you had to take some responsibility too and I wanted to know what that would be. I guess now I know. On that note, I guess I'll have another scotch.

(KATE goes and pours another scotch.)

CHARLIE

Kate, we don't direct life. It just happens. I'm just a guest in what we call life. I go where it takes me and it's not even reality.

KATE

And I suppose if you don't recognize life as reality, you don't have to take responsibility?

CHARLIE

Remember "The Prophet"? Becky was looking for it today. She reminded me about the quote that "children are living arrows that are sent forth." You know it, you quote it to the kids enough. Now, Kahlil Gibran doesn't imply there is responsibility. Once they are shot into the air, they are their own beings.

KATE

Yes, but that was about children and realizing they had their own destinies to fulfill . We are talking about your mother. You can't equate your mother with our children.

CHARLIE

Why not? She's childlike. She has managed without us. She's fulfilling her own destiny.

KATE

Charlie, I can't argue this with you. Our children are grown, they make up their minds and live with the consequences. Your mother has lost her mind; someone has to make choices for her and take the responsibility for her existence.

CHARLIE

I know that Kate. God knows, I want to bring her back into some kind of reality that I can recognize so that we can communicate. I can't move into the reality she is living in. So, I have to bring her to mine. (Pause) I love my mother, but I don't know her. My dad abandoned us when

I was fourteen. I got a night job, she was working, we didn't see each other. I went to night school to get my degree. We saw each other less. It's been less and less throughout the years. I don't know if I can fill in the spaces, even if I do get her mind back.

KATE

Well, Charlie, I hope you're successful. I hope you aren't disappointed.

CHARLIE
(Contemplatively - going back to his book.)
You know, I was thinking the other day that if we were made in the image of God, then God had to have electrons, neutrons and protons and if that's the case, then the composition of those must vary in God the Father, God the Son and God the Holy Spirit. Now that makes sense.

KATE

Jesus H. Christ, Charlie, would you get your head out of your neurons and synapses and realize we have a dying woman on our hands?
(Kate storms out of the room.)

CHARLIE
(Yelling after her.)
Kate... Kate... Kate don't you know. Nothing dies. Life and death are one, like yin and yang. Like the river flowing into the sea.

(Lights dim to black.)

ACT I

Scene IV

(At Rise: Several days later. It is Saturday morning. Setting is the same with debris etc. but rocking chair has been moved to left front of stage.)

(CASEY and ERIC are standing at the kitchen bar mixing brownies in a bowl, from a boxed mix. BECKY has entered with a box of clothes she's going to take with her.)

BECKY

Alice B. Toklas brownies?

CASEY

Yeah.

ERIC
(Pours the grass in from a plastic bag.)

BECKY

Aren't you Casey's friend Eric?

ERIC

Yeah, you the oldest sister?

BECKY

No, I'm Becky.

ERIC

I get you guys all mixed up.

BECKY

Lissa is the oldest girl. She's gay and she lives out west.

ERIC

Oh, that's right, she teaches deaf and blind kids. I didn't know she was gay.

CASEY

Yeah, well, I think Becky is the only one that has problems with that. It doesn't bother the rest of us.

BECKY

Well, I just don't understand it.

CASEY

You should be glad she's not heterosexual and isn't around to compete for your John's.

ERIC

How are you getting along with your John?

BECKY
(Brushing off the subject.)

We're doing just fine, thank you. (Beat) Hey are you making those with your stash or Austin's?

CASEY

Mine, naturally. I don't wanna die young.

> (ENTER AUSTIN dressed in a suit with brief case. ERIC backs away.)

AUSTIN

Hey,

> (Ignoring ERIC, sticks his fingers in mix.)

Alice B's?

CASEY

Yeah, and it's my stash. Man, what is it with you. Nothing exists for you except drugs.

ERIC

(Uneasily)

Hey Case I think I'd better be goin'. Save one for me okay?

CASEY

You don't have to go. Okay. I'll save one.

(EXIT ERIC)

BECKY

I'll see you later.

> (To AUSTIN who is still dipping into the batter.)

I hear Jenny said that you were such a nice young man because you dress up and go out to work every day.

AUSTIN

Yeah, it's the brief case.

CASEY

That makes you legitimate?

AUSTIN

Well, at least I'm not livin' off Mother and Father and bringing strays home.

CASEY

Oh yeah, I don't see you paying any rent.

AUSTIN

I'm saving my money. One of my buddies just bought a house and land and a beautiful speedboat.

CASEY

A boat bought with speed... that's irony. How is the drug trade these days?

AUSTIN

(Pause)

It's great! It's risky but, it pays a hell of a lot better than being a short order cook.

BECKY

(With interest.)

Got any good coke?

AUSTIN

As a matter of fact, I'll get some in today. Want some, Casey?

CASEY

No. Grass is good enough for me. Besides, I see you looking at that old lady in there and you're gonna blow your mind, just like hers. Just give you a year or two.

AUSTIN

Shut your Goddam mouth.

CASEY

You know, Jenny thinks her son is twenty-eight and Dad is trying to act like twenty-eight, but you are twenty-eight. I'll betcha she thinks you are her son and that's why she likes you.

AUSTIN

Casey, I don't want to hear any more. Understand?

BECKY

Austin, how come you offered Casey the coke when I'm the one who wants it?

AUSTIN

Oh, you always WANT it.

CASEY

I see your face when you look at her and you're scared.

AUSTIN

Listen you motherfu…

BECKY
(Interrupts)
That's all right Austin, it runs in the family. You and I will do our coke and turn out wandering around in a daze like Jenny. And Dad.

AUSTIN

Leave Father out of it.

CASEY

"Father". " Mother". You always sound like your looking down your nose at the rest of us.

43

(CASEY is pouring batter in pans and puts them in the oven. KATE ENTERS living room supporting JENNY and leading her to the chair. Once seated, KATE picks up a few papers and heads for the crowd in the kitchen. She begins to wash some dishes.
CHARLIE ENTERS from the hall with his short tennis shorts on, his boxer shorts hanging lower than his tennis shorts and his tennis racket in hand wearing a childish expression and demonstrating a youthful demeanor and addresses JENNY.)

CHARLIE

Hi, Mom, I'm going out to play tennis. Want to come with me? Do you remember how I played tennis as a kid? (Pause) I still play. In Florida I can play all year round. Well, I really have to practice my back swing. Maybe sometime you'll want to come and watch me.

JENNY
(Looks up in amazement and confusion.)
Who are you?

CHARLIE

I'm Charles, your son. I always used to play tennis. Can you picture me when I was about… oh, twenty? I think you remember me being younger, but we haven't seen each other for a number of years. I'm much older now.   I'm sure you'll remember me better after you get settled here.
(Hesitantly)
I'm sure.

(CHARLIE pats her on the head and EXITS.)

JENNY
(Speaks to an empty room.)
I'm a registered nurse, you know. I'm a registered nurse.

KATE
(Washing dishes in kitchen.)
God, I left your Dad to put her to bed last night, and he just put her pajamas on over her daytime clothes.

CASEY

He didn't.

KATE

Oh yes he did.
(Pause)
Oh Becky, is it ok, I mean about your staying with John?

BECKY

Yeah. I've been staying there. I just have to move some more of my stuff in.

CASEY

Which John?

AUSTIN

Becky stays with any John that will have her.

BECKY

I don't prostitute myself any more than you do Austin, we both can be bought. Besides. I like this John, its John Fairchild. He's nice.

(EXIT BECKY to get some more clothes to put in the box.)

KATE

I want you to leave Becky alone. I slept my way clear across Europe before I met your father, back in the days when I was young and beautiful, and vital.

CASEY

Ahhh, was that in the Mesozoic or Paleolithic age.

(Kate shoots him a grimace.)

What did you do in those days check out the male dinosaurs?

KATE

You're cute.
                    (Playfully)
Well, let's see after I got my Bachelor's in Economics I worked in New York as a Labor Union organizer. I was always concerned about the blue-collar worker. Later, I worked on an exchange student project where we even brought Nazi youths over to let them see what a democracy was really like. Then, all my friends took off for Europe so I got together enough money to follow them. I met a French aeronautical engineer on the boat and he gave me a job. So, when I arrived in Paris, I had a job as his chauffeur. How about that?

CASEY

Wow! Did you get any tickets?

KATE

As a matter of fact I did but his ex-wife was having an affair with the mayor of Paris, and they were still good friends, so between the two of them, I got all my tickets fixed.

CASEY

Pretty cool! Did you stay with your friends?

KATE

Yeah, we lived in this run down hotel, the Pax. It was fun. We never knew who we were coming home to. There was a gun runner from Morocco, an architect from England, lots of interesting people.
                    (KATE flourishes her drink.)

Ou la la. Vive Paris and Vive L'amour.

AUSTIN

Dad says you were a virgin when he married you.

KATE

Virgin, hell. I would never marry anyone I hadn't slept with.
Now, you speak of virginity, your dad was a virgin until he was 34.

AUSTIN

How come... 34? Are you sure?

KATE

Yes. The way he tells it, when he was thirty-three trying to live a good Christian life and he found out that he wasn't going to be the next Jesus Christ, he decided to learn to drink, swear, and screw. I think he learned it in that order.

CASEY

God! I hope that doesn't run in the family. The virginity, that is.

AUSTIN

You still a virgin?

CASEY

You know Austin, as the youngest in this family I've learned to keep my private life private, especially with sisters and brothers.

AUSTIN

Are you gay like Lissa?

CASEY

No, I'm not gay. I have a girl friend. I have several girl friends but believe me, you would be the last one to know anything personal about my love life.

KATE

(Pauses as she continues puttering around kitchen in a semi-daze.)

That woman is gonna drive me crazy.

CASEY

You mean Jenny?

KATE

Who else? Now she wants me to sleep with her. She's afraid of sleeping alone.

CASEY

So what did you tell her?

KATE

I told her I had enough problems sleeping with her son, much less his mother.

CASEY

Oh Mom, you didn't.

(KATE ignores CASEY. BECKY ENTERS with more clothes.)

BECKY

Stick around, Casey's got some Alice B. brownies in the oven have one you'll feel better, Mom.

(KATE still in a state starts to leave when phone rings. KATE answers. A pinpoint light appears at side of stage and LISSA appears on phone.)

KATE

Yes, we'll accept the charges. Lissa... How are you. What's happening?

LISSA

We're fine. Leslie and I found a nice little house to rent. What's going on there and how's Jenny?

KATE

(Pause)

Oh we're okay, just going a little crazy.

> (KATE reaches under counter to pour herself a scotch.
> CASEY mouths WATER?
> KATE mouths back no STRAIGHT.
> CASEY shakes head in mock chastisement.
> BECKY leans over counter. She wants to talk to LISSA.
> AUSTIN EXITS through hall.)

LISSA

So what are you going to do with her? Are you sure you can deal with this?

KATE

Well, we don't know what we're going to do. We're going to have to do something with her. No, I can't handle it... Would you believe that now she is afraid of sleeping alone and wants me to sleep with her?

> (Pause. Then laughter. KATE grabs her crotch upsets scotch. She can't control her bladder. BECKY grabs phone.)

BECKY

What did you say to her? She's peeing all over the kitchen floor...You what?

> (BECKY laughing.)

CASEY

What'd she say?

BECKY

(Laughing hard.)

She told Mom "what the old girl needs is sex so she suggests we get her a girl friend."

Oh God, Lissa. She's so old. You should see her.

(BECKY continues talking to LISSA while CASEY automatically gets floor mop and starts mopping up after his mother.)

KATE
(Grabs phone from BECKY.)
I'll talk to you some other time. I gotta change my pants.
(Gives phone back to BECKY.)
Tell her that's what happens when you've had five kids.

(EXIT KATE)
BECKY

Did you hear that? Mom,
(BECKY yells after KATE.)
Lissa says most lesbians don't have that trouble.
(Hear KATE laughing.)
Hey, Lissa, why don't you call me at 449-9003, that's John's number.

LISSA
Is this an old John or a new John?

BECKY
A new John. I like him. Well, at any rate we can talk there I'm leaving in a few minutes. Gotta get some clothes, call in about 30 minutes… make it an hour.
Okay? Okay.

(AUSTIN ENTERS with brief case.)

I thought you'd left. Here, talk to Lissa.
(Hands phone to AUSTIN.)

(BECKY EXITS)

AUSTIN
(With disinterest.)

Hi, Lissa. How's your sex life?

LISSA

It's on a high. and without drugs. How's yours or do you remember anything about it?

AUSTIN

Hey, I don't need your shit. I'm doing fine. Why don't you talk to Casey.
(Hands phone to CASEY.)

CASEY

Lissa, don't pay any attention to him. He's just his normal bullying self. How's your job?

LISSA

Let me tell you what happened today. This new little Mexican boy, who's deaf and partially blind, came into my room and asked if I was Miss Feisty Kraus.

CASEY

Oh God, that's funny. What did you say?

LISSA

I signed to him if he knew the meaning of "feisty" and he said, "I think it must mean beautiful." Then he asked me if I'd marry him.

CASEY

Oh gee, you're lucky he can't see well. Those kids don't know what a bitch you can be.

LISSA

That's good Casey, Beauty and the Bitch. You know, I tell the kids stories about my family and they all roar. They can't believe you guys are real.

CASEY

Well, who says we are.

(AUSTIN waves him to hang up the phone.)
Ah, Lissa, Austin is waiting for some brownies I have in the oven he
wants me to hang up.

LISSA

Let me talk to him.
(CASEY hands the phone to AUSTIN who takes it
reluctantly.)
Austin, are you still playing the "oldest" in the family routine, still
threatening and pushing everyone around?

AUSTIN

Lissa, I don't want to listen to you, or talk to you.

(ENTER BECKY with box of clothes.)

LISSA

You bastard, leave them alone. You are such a shit… you are.

AUSTIN

Goodbye, Lissa.
(She continues.)
Goodbye, Lissa,
(He slams the receiver down.)
God, she's a pain in the ass. Now where's that brownie?

(CASEY takes the pan from the oven. AUSTIN takes
one brownie and eats it and proceeds to take two
more.)

(ENTER BYRON)

BYRON
(To BECKY)
Need your clothes moved over to John's? I gotta truck.

AUSTIN

A truck?

BYRON

Yeah, a truck.
(Ignoring AUSTIN.)
This woman who works with me at the library gave me her truck.

BECKY

Gave it to you!

BYRON

Well, actually I've been dating her for a while. Her name's Cathy. She's an older woman, you might say, but she's lonesome and kind of shy and so am I, so we kind of fit each other.

CASEY

So?

BYRON

So, she wants to keep me.

AUSTIN

She's got lousy taste.

BYRON
(Ignoring AUSTIN.)
Well, I didn't say I was going to, but I figured if you didn't have a guy to stay with, that I could manage this and besides I think it might be good for me anyway. So, I'm gonna move in with her. for a little while. That's why I have the truck.

BECKY

That's okay. Actually, I really like this John,
(Picking up the box of clothes.)

but you can drive me over to his place. (Sigh) It's just that I get so I like a guy... then I find out what a shit he is... and... all I want to do is get married and have kids! Maybe I'll just get old and OD...

(Handing Byron the box of clothes.)

(As BECKY and BYRON EXIT they pass JENNY in her chair.)

BYRON

Depressing, isn't it?

BECKY

I feel sorry for her.

BYRON

Yeah, me too.

JENNY

I'm a professional nurse, you know.

BECKY and BYRON

Yes, Jenny, we know.

(BYRON pats JENNY on the head as they EXIT. AUSTIN EXITS too, still eating his brownies. Lights lower and CASEY EXITS. Pin light spot on JENNY who rocks and croons. ENTER CHARLIE, body sagging, tennis racket in hand, he approaches JENNY's chair and kneels down.)

CHARLIE

Mother. Mother, look at me. Do you remember when I used to play tennis? I was a kid.

(JENNY looks blankly at him.)

Mother, share your thoughts with me. What are you thinking about?

JENNY

I had two chickens, Sophie and Christopher. They used to walk down to the fence with me every day when I went to school. They were such good friends.

CHARLIE

Mother, look at me. Remember me? I'm your son Charlie.

JENNY

Charlie? Charlie?

CHARLIE

(With a touch of hope.)

Mother.

(CHARLIE runs to the kitchen and gets two drumsticks from the refrigerator.)

Mother... Look... this is Sophie

(He quickly eats one drumstick.)

and this is Christopher.

(He eats the other and throws them on the floor.)

They are gone... just like that, but I'm here. Yes, Mother...I'm alive, I'm Charlie, your son.

JENNY

I don't know a Charlie. I have a son. His name is Charles and he has impeccable table manners. He's young.

CHARLIE

How young, Mother?

JENNY

Oh, very young. Maybe, 28.

CHARLIE

Mother, please ... Remember when I went to school?

JENNY

I'm not your mother. My son is young.

CHARLIE

Mother!

> (CHARLIE runs into the next room and comes out with his college diploma.)

Mother, remember when I graduated from college?

JENNY

College? I never graduated from college, but I'm a registered nurse, you know.

CHARLIE

Yes, I know.

> (Trying to think of another tactic.)

Mother... remember when I was fourteen and my father abandoned us?

JENNY

My Father, Mother, God, would never abandon his children. NEVER!

CHARLIE

Oh, Mother! Please Dear God... let her know me.... Please! Please! Please!

> (CHARLIE puts his head down and quietly sobs.)

JENNY

God is my friend... Jesus is my friend... what a friend we have in Jesus.

CHARLIE

> (Almost screaming.)

MOTHER!

(CHARLIE rises slowly, kisses her on the forehead ... and with a sense of utter defeat, EXITS.)

(The lights are lowered until there is just a pinpoint of light on JENNY.)

JENNY
(Sings)
We are going down the valley one by one

With our faces toward the setting sun

One by one the cares of life forever pass

And we shall stand upon the riverbank at last.

(Lights to black.)

ACT II

Scene I

(Time: Two Months Later.)

(At Rise: Living room. Low lights. JENNY is asleep in rockin chair. CHARLIE is sitting in over stuffed chair in reverie.)

(ENTER KATE in a rush.)

KATE

Oh … I've gotta get a drink. You want one?

CHARLIE

Got one.

KATE

Charlie, we have to talk.
   (KATE brings drink in and plops in another chair, she
   takes a big gulp and a deep breath.)
I gotta job.

CHARLIE

A job! That's nice.

KATE

It was offered to me today. I figured the kids are all grown even though they're still hanging around. I'll be Assistant Coordinator of the Head-start Program for the county.

CHARLIE

My wife, the professional.

KATE

Don't make fun.

CHARLIE

I'm not making fun. If you want a job, I think you should have a job.

KATE

I'm scared as hell to go back to work after all these years, but I'm excited too. I think I'll like it. I just hope I do a good job. You know, Charlie, when they offered it to me today, it was like. I don't know, like stepping out in the sun. I said "yes". It requires a Masters Degree. I'm qualified, and it's 8 to 5. I could afford someone to come in and clean once a week.

CHARLIE

Oh, what an un-full-filling job for someone!

KATE
(With a flash of anger.)
But there's Jenny.

CHARLIE

So.

KATE

Is that all you have to say?

CHARLIE

I figure you've got that all worked out too.

KATE

Charlie, it's been two months. In that time I've found I'm no caretaker. It's different taking care of children. I'm tired of putting her clothes on, buttoning, zipping, and bathing that old body. I'm tired. I need to be me or something.

CHARLIE

Okay.

KATE

I figure we could have someone come in. Or, there's a daycare center for senior citizens a few blocks away from where I work.

CHARLIE

Do whatever you think is best.

KATE

Charlie ... you've given up.

CHARLIE

Our days are numbered like the hairs of our head ... I'm not going to split hairs, hell, I can't afford to.
(Rubbing his thinning hair.)

KATE

I don't understand you. One minute you're trying to make yourself 28 years old so that you can bring your mother's mind back to reality; the next minute you're acting as if she is dead. What is this?

CHARLIE

I don't know. I vacillate. I look at her and my scientific mind says she's lost her mind, therefore, she's dead. I look at her again and my Christian Science mind says, as long as she's breathing there's a chance.

KATE

Charlie, you know your scientific mind doesn't say she's dead. It's your intellectual snob-ism. You figure anyone who loses their mind must be dead, but scientifically, you know better.

CHARLIE

Look, Kate, I really don't want to discuss this. I have to work it out. I was sure, if I could find out what year she was living in I could replicate it, make it happen and slowly bring her back. I can't. I don't know what else to do. I don't want to do anything.

KATE

Charlie, she's your mother. You have to do something. Don't make me take total responsibility for this decision or any others.

CHARLIE

(Irritated)

What the hell do you want, Kate? I sired your children, I provide for the family and I service you on a regular basis.

KATE

You WHAT?

(Furious)

You service me? You think you are some kind of maintenance mechanic? You take your hose … give me a lube job … fill me up? Well, let me tell you, mister master- mind, you're anything but high octane.

CHARLIE

Why are you so upset? That's what men do. They propagate and perpetuate.

KATE

They are also supposed to take responsibility or is that word just not in your vast vocabulary? Or does your responsibility begin and end with your prick?

CHARLIE

Well,

(Thoughtfully looking at it.)
you might have something there. We perpetuate the species that way, we have to have the balls to go out and bring home the essentials… and we have to provide the sexual pleasures that keep our spouses happy.

KATE

Oh God! Sometimes I wonder what I ever saw in you.

CHARLIE

Maybe that's why all men are bow-legged. They all are, you know, to some extent.

KATE

I think you've lost your fucking mind!

CHARLIE

No, really, it's the balls. Without them we'd be nothing.
(Using a small round table by the chair, he puts his legs up on and around it.)
So, we put them into a boney, protective, parentheses … that's what makes us bow-legged. Ever notice jocks … the bigger the balls the more bow-legged.

(KATE walks around in amazement.)

KATE

(Yelling)
Goddam it, Charlie!

CHARLIE

Of course, if you did Yoga you could put your legs around your head.
(Trying to do it.)
Maybe that's the difference between Eastern and Western Philosophy…
they think the mind is worth protecting.

KATE

Get your head out from up your ass and let the light of reality in.

CHARLIE

Now, that's physically impossible... not even a good Yogi could do that.

(Putting his legs down.)

KATE

Oh, am I glad we had this talk. I am so glad I took that job and I am sick and tired of your contrived mind trips to get you out of having to make decisions or participate in anything.

(CHARLIE is still contemplating.)

Charlie,

(KATE goes over and yells in his ear.)

Your mother... we have to do something about YOUR mother ... she is YOURS.

(KATE walks over and pours more scotch in her drink. KATE then moves apart and a single spot may be used to highlight her while the other lights are lowered.)

I feel guilty and she's not my mother. I know I'm walking out on her, so to speak. I don't like to admit I can't handle something.

(Pause)

Having her here, I realize that I've walked out on myself. I've been a mother for so long, I almost forgot about the me that lived and worked in New York... in Paris. I just can't stay home anymore and watch that old lady die. I see myself sitting in that rocking chair. I hate old age. Her body's so wrinkled. I hate bathing her and looking at her because I see me. I just hope I die before I ever get where she's at. I desperately want to be young ... I want to be like my kids ... but I feel myself dying.

(She touches her face and her arms.)

So, I turn to you because ... because I don't like this guilt... and she is YOUR mother.

(CHARLIE stands up and moves toward a spot away from KATE, the lights stay low the pinpoint spot on KATE goes off and one appears on CHARLIE.)

CHARLIE

She's not my mother. She doesn't know me. She knows chickens.
(He walks to the refrigerator and takes out a drumstick and bites into it.)
She remembers Christopher and Sophie two guinea hens that walked her down to the fence when she went to school.
(Voice breaks.)
It's her mind. God, to lose your mind... I tried to be young ... I tried to move her into the present. Why can't it work?

(Suddenly CHARLIE becomes aware he's been talking in a revealing manner. Spot is out and lights come up a little. He turns back to KATE.)

Kate, my arrow has fallen to earth. Maybe in another life, maybe in another time, some other woman will shoot me into the air.

(KATE moves hesitantly over to CHARLIE and puts her arm around him.)

KATE

Charlie, I'm sorry you've had to go through this. I'm sorry you want to run away from it ... but the reality is ... she's not going to get her mind back.
(KATE walks away and a spot follows her there is now a spot on CHARLIE.)

CHARLIE

Not to remember ... is a living death.

KATE

My body... look at it...

CHARLIE

My mind ... not to be able to use it...

KATE

No way to stop it ... my feet hurt ... I get so tired ... I

(KATE and CHARLIE turn toward each other.)

BOTH

I guess... it's the daycare center.

(The two spots come together as CHARLIE and KATE move together. They put their arms around each other. He offers her a bite of the drumstick and they move to EXIT through the hall. Spots dim to black and a pinpoint light comes up on JENNY's rocking chair and we see JENNY has awakened and sings in a voice a little Younger than in ACT I.)

JENNY

We are going down the valley, one by one

With our faces toward the setting sun

One by one the cares of life forever pass

And we shall stand upon the riverbank at last.

(Lights dim to black.)

ACT II

Scene II

(Time: Next day.)

(Setting: Living room.)

JENNY
(Humming to self.)

(ENTER BYRON)

BYRON
Hi Jenny.

JENNY
I'm a registered nurse, you know.

BYRON
Oh, Jenny, did you say you're feeling worse, you know?

JENNY
(Like a child chastised.)
I'm a registered nurse, you know.

BYRON

Did you say you were in a hearse, you know? Or did you say life is a curse, you know?

> (JENNY looks at BYRON as he moves away from her chair toward left of center stage. Pinpoint light over JENNY's head dims. Follow spot picks up BYRON's movements and when he reaches Spot on stage.)

(To self)
Why did you do that … that's like stepping on an innocent bug. Oh, I've got to get out of here … like Lissa. I must really hate myself to be that cruel.

> (Lights dim and pinpoint spot is on JENNY in chair. BRYON turns around and goes to sit on the floor at the foot of JENNY's chair.)

BYRON

Oh, Jenny. I'm so sorry. It's not your fault. I live in this dark hole in my head. (Pause) The doctor says I have depression.
(Pause – body rock.)
Sometimes I look at you and wish we could exchange places. At least you're able to forget… and the things around you don't seem to matter.
(Beat)
I wonder if you dream. Or maybe everything is a dream to you.
(Pause)
I dream every night. (Pause) I dream the same dream every night.
(Pause)
I dream about a little boy who loves to visit a pretty glade in the woods. He sits there and just meditates and lets it all go. One day he plants little bamboo trees all around the glade. Each day he spends more and more time there until finally he spends most of his time there. Then, one day when he stops meditating, he looks up at his bamboo and sees that is has grown tall and thick and he can't get out of the bamboo wall…

(BYRON seems to come of out his reverie.)

JENNY
(Looks at him as if trying to understand.)
I'm a registered nurse, you know.

BYRON
Yes, I know. I just wish you could heal me. I wish you could give me the courage to want to live … but in a way, I think you already helped me.

(He pats her hand.)

(Pinpoint light dims. Lights up as BECKY ENTERS. She sees BYRON, goes over, pats him on the head and sits on the couch.)

BYRON
What's the matter?

BECKY
I've got problems.

BYRON
Big ones?

BECKY
Big and little.

BYRON
You want to talk?

BECKY
I've got to see Mom.

BYRON
You pregnant?

BECKY

How'd you know?

BYRON

There aren't too many problems that can be both big and little at the same time. When did you find out?

BECKY

About a week ago, but I was afraid to tell Mom. I told Lissa because I needed to tell someone. I've talked to her a couple of times.

BYRON

What are you going to do?

BECKY

We're gonna get married.

BYRON

Is that what you want?

BECKY

I think so. But now, that I'm right up to it … I'm not sure. I mean, I want the baby and I care more for John than I have for anyone.

BYRON

Sounds reasonable - not lovable.

BECKY

(BECKY gets up and moves right of center stage.)

I'm not sure love exists. I just see life as a series of days where you create each day as you go along. Ma always said that having us was her most creative effort, but I wonder how she feels about her creation now… and what about our creations? Oh God, I wonder what the drugs will do? That's what really worries me.

BYRON

How far along are you?

BECKY

Two months. I've done some coke ... and grass, of course. Now that I know I'm pregnant, I'm cutting back ... but it's hard. No coke ... but I still do a little grass every day. It relaxes me ... Oh God, I wonder what I'm carrying.
(Starts to cry.)
I just want it to be okay. I should be able to quit completely in a week or two ... it's all so hard.

BYRON

How's John feel about the baby?

BECKY

I'm not sure, I mean, he wants the baby... I think, almost as much as I do, but, well ... it's the responsibility.
(She moves over to couch.)
He doesn't exactly have a steady job.

BYRON

What's exactly?

BECKY

Exactly is exactly what Austin does.

BYRON

Push drugs? That figures!

BECKY

You don't know. He's a lot older than I am and he's a Vietnam Vet. He was just a kid when he went to war. A farm boy. He can grow anything. I guess he got so scared over there. He still has nightmares. Drugs were the only thing that took the hell out of the war for him. Well, now he's addicted and so he grows some grass and sells the hard stuff. I don't think he is a courier like Austin. I really don't know much about the business. We don't talk about it.

(Pause)

So, what do you think?

BYRON

It's your choice. Life is choice. Some people make few choices so that they limit the odds. Some people make lots of them and then spend the rest of their lives trying to remedy the bad ones ... and some people, like me, are too afraid to make any.

BECKY

You chose not to register for the selective service.

BYRON

Yeah, so I'm against war, but I don't know whether it was a choice or cowardice.

(Beat)

But I have made a choice. I'm getting married.

(ENTER KATE)

BECKY

Married? You?

KATE

You're doing WHAT?

BYRON

Mom, I'm getting married. I don't know if it's right ... but I've got to get out of here. Cathy's gonna take me out west and send me back to school.

She's a really nice person, gentle, quiet. You'll like her.

She needs me. She doesn't think anyone could love her.

KATE

Cathy, like me. Katherine.

BYRON

But she spells hers with a "C".

KATE

Byron, don't you think you should give it some time. Like at least a few months?

BYRON

Time is all I've given life. No action. Now I'm taking action.

KATE

Well, it's your life. I'm sure she's nice.
        (Pause)
I know you need someone. I just hope you really care for each other, it helps.

(KATE walks over and hugs him.)

BYRON

Did you and Dad really care for each other?

KATE

Did? Past tense? We still do, but differently now. When we met we were older than most. I was 27; he was 39. Both of us wanted a home and family right away. I was fascinated by his mind and he was enamored of my body. Now I realize how little of life revolves around how smart you are, and my body isn't what it used to be. You might say we've evolved into two people who share each other's inadequacies. We have created too much personal history to get a divorce, even though we've considered it. We are two people who have decided to live our own lives, but do it together. (Beat)
I'm sure Cathy's nice. I know you need someone. everybody does. I just … I just… I'm so surprised, I don't know what to say.

(KATE ponders briefly as she wanders around the kitchen, what more she should say. BECKY who has been watching gets up and shakes KATE's arm.)

BECKY

Mom ... Mom ... I'm pregnant.

KATE

Oh great!
(She hugs BECKY.)
It's all right ... it's all right, honey. You've always wanted a baby and it looks like we're all going to have one. Right? Right.
(Answering her own question and a bit flustered.)
That, I've been expecting to some extent, but Byron. Well, I guess we're going to have a baby and a wedding.
(Looking at Becky.)
Or is it two weddings?

(BECKY nods yes. BYRON gets up to join them and KATE puts her arms around both of them.)
Well, come on, let's have a drink. Let's have three drinks. Oh hell, let's just tie one on.
(KATE starts pulling glasses out of the cupboard and getting the booze out.)
Now, when am I going to meet Cathy?

BYRON

How about next weekend?

BECKY

That's great, because John and I are going to get married next weekend. I told Lissa last week that we would get married this weekend and she said she would come home for it.

KATE

You told Lissa?
(Pause)

Next weekend?

>(Pause)

Where?

BECKY

Here.

KATE

Here? In this house?
>(Looking around.)

Well, I guess that's okay. What about John's parents?

BECKY

They approve, but they won't be able to get here. We figured we might drive out west to see them. Kind of like a honeymoon.

KATE

Well, that's all right then. I won't have to have the place spotless. Oh, don't tell me you're getting married next weekend too, Byron.

BYRON

Naw, it'll probably be a couple of months for us. We gotta work a few things out.

KATE

Okay. Well, here's to a new adventure for both of you … and for me too. I've got a job.

BECKY

A job?   But Mom, I thought you would be around to be a grandmother!

KATE

I'm ready to be me. I'm ready to get out of here and into the world again. I'm not too sure I'm ready to be a grandmother.

BECKY

But Mom, won't it be wonderful to have a little one running around calling you "Grandma"?

KATE

Grandma? No. Kate? Yes.

BECKY

Oh, okay.
                    (A little surprised and disappointed.)
If that's what you want!

KATE

I'm so excited. I only have to work half days the first week. We're going to put Jenny in a Daycare Center. Oh, I feel wonderful.
                    (Beat)
Now, how far along are you?

BECKY

About two months.

KATE

Okay, and Cathy, just how much older is she?

BYRON

Don't tell her I told you, but about ten years.

KATE

I wouldn't say anything about it. After all, your Dad is twelve years older than I am and I'm 58 … or is it 57? Oh, well, come on, let's drink up and get mellow. We have a lot of good reasons.
                    (KATE pours more liquor in glasses.
                    ENTER CASEY running.)

CASEY

Mom… Mom … Austin … they got Austin.

KATE

Who?

CASEY

The cops.
> (Trying to catch his breath.)

They called Dad, and he didn't know how to get to the jail so I put my bike in the car and went with him. He's still there. He told me to tell you not to worry, he thinks he can get Austin released into his custody, and if not, he'll put up the bail.

> (KATE gets up and heads for the kitchen.)

KATE

Time to drink. You guys get your own…
> (Sighs, then looks over at JENNY in the chair.)

Jenny, you want a drink?

BECKY

SHH. She's asleep.
> (KATE brings a drink back from the kitchen. Everyone is drinking and listening to CASEY.)

CASEY

I don't know how it happened. I guess a drug deal was going down and they got him. They really didn't let Dad talk to him. I just know I've never seen Austin look so bad.

KATE

Well, this, at least is no surprise. I'm just amazed it hasn't happened sooner.
> (Beat)

I hope Charlie can get him released. He's got to be here for the wedding.

CASEY

Wedding!

KATE

Yes.

BECKY

Yeah, John and I are getting married next weekend.

CASEY

Pregnant?

BECKY

How'd you know?

CASEY

Difficult deduction.

BECKY

And Lissa's coming home for it. She'll be home this week, she says.

CASEY

I don't think the world's ready for this ... I know it's not ready for Lissa.
I think I need a drink too, Ma.

(CASEY moves to kitchen to pour a drink.)

BYRON

Yeah, and I'm getting married too ... but not next weekend.

CASEY

That calls for a double shot. What the hell's gotten into everybody?
All of a sudden everybody's leaving home.

(ENTER CHARLIE and AUSTIN)

CHARLIE

It's okay. You're okay.
                (To Austin)

If you had waited, Casey, I could have brought you home. He's okay Kate. He can stay at home until the trial.

AUSTIN

(Crying)
Mom, I'm sorry ... I'll never do it again ... I'm sorry ... I'm so sorry.

KATE

(Holding him.)
What are you sorry for?

AUSTIN

I'm sorry ...

KATE

Sorry you got caught? Austin, we told you ...

AUSTIN

I know ... I know ...

KATE

But you didn't believe us.

AUSTIN

I thought I was being careful.

KATE

So you're only sorry you got caught. You're not sorry that you pushed drugs ... sold drugs ... took drugs?

AUSTIN

I'm sorry I disappointed you and Fa... Dad.

KATE

It's your life, not ours - your decision, not ours - your consequence, not ours. Don't you care about your life?

AUSTIN

I

(Crying)

I ... guess not. I just know I have to come off it and I don't know if I can.

KATE

But you are.

AUSTIN

(Nods yes.)

KATE

I hope you mean that.

(She pats him on the head and rubs his back.)

CHARLIE

Oh, he means it Kate, don't you, son?

AUSTIN

(Sobbing)

I'm sorry. I'm sorry.

CASEY

Hey, take it easy, man. You're at home. It's not as if we don't understand.

AUSTIN

Yeah, but you always said ... I would blow my mind.

CASEY

(Interrupts)

Yeah, well, forget what I said.

(CASEY starts looking around to find the basketball. BECKY goes over and pats AUSTIN's shoulder.)

BECKY

Don't worry, they'll probably let you off with some community work. After all, it's your first time.

BYRON

Hey, one of my friends was caught with probably a lot more than you had and he just had to work at a city park for a few weeks cleaning it up and planting shrubs. That's not so bad.

AUSTIN

You don't understand. I have to quit. Do you know what you go through? I don't know if ... I ... can without going crazy. I tried it one weekend and I thought I was going to die.

CHARLIE

You can do it. You know, death is an integral part of progress. The past has to die to give you the momentum to move on. This is an important time in your life, son.

BECKY

Yeah, and you'll make it.

BYRON

And we'll help.

CASEY
(Finding the basketball.)
Yeah, you can play some ball with me. It'll help you get rid of the tension.
                    (Bounces it to AUSTIN who doesn't catch it but covers his ears.)

AUSTIN

It hurts my head.

KATE

Well, nobody is going to do anything right now except eat. Come on, Austin. Charlie, you too.

(EXIT KATE to kitchen and BECKY follows.)
(ENTER ERIC)

ERIC

Hey everyone, what's goin' on?

KATE

Hi Eric, come on and get something to eat.

(ERIC heads for kitchen.)

Remember, all of you, tomorrow is my first day of work and Jenny's first time in daycare. I'll take her. Charlie, you pick her up. Is she still asleep?

CHARLIE

Yes she is.

KATE

Well, we'll feed her later, I guess.

CASEY

Hey, get a load of the executive …issuing orders already.

(AUSTIN, CHARLIE, KATE, BECKY, look for food in the refrigerator.
CASEY bounces the ball and EXITS with them.
BYRON pulls at CHARLIE's arm as he is about to follow.
All lights are dimmed and a pinpoint spot is up on CHARLIE and BYRON.)

BYRON

Dad. I wanted to say something to you.

CHARLIE

Say what?

BYRON

I was talking to Jenny today.

CHARLIE

Oh! What did she say?

BYRON

She didn't. She listened. I realized, she didn't know what I was saying, but the mere fact that I actually expressed how I felt, helped me. You know the Docs all tell me that I repress all my feelings, that's why I get so depressed.

CHARLIE

Doctors.

BYRON

Well, I'm trying to turn my life around.

CHARLIE

And talking to Jenny is the first step?

BYRON

No, talking to you is the first big step. You see, they always tell me I'm like you and I don't want to be like you. I know this probably isn't the time to tell you this, what with Austin's problems, but if I don't do it now, I might never do it.

CHARLIE

Well tell me. I think you should be yourself, not me.

BYRON

That's true, but I see myself in you. You know, you always sit back and look at us like a lion surveying your offspring. When you come home from work you head for your room, watch television, or play chess on the computer. We have to come to you; you never reach out to us.

CHARLIE

And you resent that.

BYRON

Yes. I've wanted to talk with you lots of times but when we talk it's as if it's an academic lecture with you knowing all things and I don't think you're that smart.

CHARLIE

Well I must admit, I have always thought because I was the oldest, I must therefore be the wisest, but I guess that doesn't hold.

BYRON

If only you would listen, if only you would reach out to us.

CHARLIE

Sometimes it's too late to reach out.   Look at Austin.
   (Lowering his voice.)
Look at Jenny.

BYRON

Dad. It's never too late to reach out. That's what I'm trying to do. I want you to know how I feel, it takes a lot of courage for me, and this is my first try.

CHARLIE

I realize that Byron, I appreciate what it took. Maybe I'm too old to learn, but I'll try.
   (Beat)
Come on, let's get some of your mother's
   (Shaking his head.)
devastating food.
   (With unfamiliarity he puts his arm around BYRON.)

   (CHARLIE and BYRON turn to go into the kitchen area with the rest. The pinpoint light is off and full lights are up. At this moment LISSA bursts through the front door.)

(ENTER LISSA)

LISSA

Hello. Where is everyone? Where was the brass band ... and the bottle of wine? Someone should have met me at the airport.

GROUP

(Except ERIC.)

LISSA!!

(Group puts food back and moves back into living room and JENNY wakes up with a start.)

KATE

Why didn't you tell us when you were coming?
(Going over to hug her.)

LISSA

(Impishly)

I wanted to surprise you.
(Beat)

Who are you?

ERIC

I'm Eric.

CASEY

Yeah, he's my friend who's staying here for a while, 'cause , 'cause his home life isn't what it should be.

LISSA

And you're staying here? Well, you've got courage and I'm impressed.
(Beat)

Speaking of impressed ... I'm gonna be an aunt!

BYRON

And a sister-in-law.

LISSA

Yeah, I know that. That's why I came home – for the wedding.

BYRON

You coming home for mine in a couple of months?

LISSA

Yours?

CHARLIE

Who's getting married?
> (Bourbon in hand.)

BYRON

Becky and I.

CHARLIE

That's incest!

KATE

Oh, I forgot that you and Austin didn't know and you too, Eric.

AUSTIN
> (Sitting on couch rocking and holding his head in his hands with drink on table.)

I hope I can be there.

LISSA

Austin, what's the matter with you?

AUSTIN

I just got out of jail.

LISSA

JAIL!
>   (Beat)

They finally got you, huh? Well, at least you're out. Mr. Big Shot must have some big shot attorneys, huh?
>   (She doesn't wait for an answer but turns her back on
>   AUSTIN who covers his head.)

Now where's Jenny? Oh there you are. I just walked right past you didn't I?

>   (LISSA walks over to JENNY's chair.)

Why do they have you stuck over here in this dark corner? My goodness,
>   (She moves the rocker out into the room.)

You have to join the party. Hi, my name is Lissa.
>   (She signs her name.)

I'm one of your granddaughters too. I know you don't remember me, but that's okay, because I don't remember you too well either. So that makes us even. I've come home to help you find a girlfriend.

JENNY

I'm a registered nurse, you know.

CASEY and KATE

Oh, God!

LISSA

Yes, I know and I also know that every woman needs a girlfriend at every stage of life and we're going to find one for you. Hey, I'm hungry. You're hungry too, aren't you? Jenny and I are hungry. Why don't you just call for some Pizzas. What kind do you like, Jenny … Pepperoni? Salami? I'll tell you what – you can have a little piece of every kind.

>   (Lissa Barks.)

Well. Who's calling?

CASEY
(At the phone.)

I am.

LISSA

Now, talk to me.
(Puts her arm around BECKY.)

Do you have a dress? Byron, is your girlfriend going to be at the wedding? Mom, can I have a drink and Austin, how in the hell did you get yourself in jail.

(To CHARLIE who has just lit up a cigar.)
Oh Dad, are you still smoking those things?

(LISSA, BYRON and BECKY EXIT.
KATE goes to the kitchen to fix a drink.
CHARLIE helps AUSTIN to his feet and they EXIT.)

CASEY
(Yelling to KATE.)

Hey Ma, Pizza's ordered. Eric and I will pick it up in about twenty minutes. We get it faster that way.

KATE

Okay.

(EXIT KATE from kitchen. ERIC moves over to JENNY's chair. CASEY stands back and watches the interaction.)

ERIC

Hey Jenny.

JENNY
(JENNY looks at him blankly.)

ERIC

I wish my grandmother lived here.
(He sits on the floor next to her.)

JENNY

(Smiling sweetly.)
Oh, I'm too young to be a grandmother.

ERIC

Yeah, I know. You're getting younger every day and I'm getting older.
(ENTER CASEY)

CASEY

She's really a great grandmother in her own way. Hey, she's going to be
a real great grandmother when Becky has her baby.

ERIC

Is Becky pregnant?

CASEY

Why do you think she's getting married so fast?

ERIC

Hey, that's great, isn't it Jenny. We need to sing a song to celebrate.
How about singing your song. I want to learn it.

(JENNY looks blankly at him, ERIC gets his guitar
which is standing against the wall.)

ERIC

Come on Jenny. How does it go? (He picks it out ...)
We are going down the valley, one by one

JENNY

With our faces toward the setting sun
(Casey joins in.)

One by one the cares of life forever pass

And we shall stand upon the riverbank at last.

CASEY

Okay Eric, now jazz it up.

ERIC
(Switching to a Jazz beat.)

We are goin' down da riva, one by one

With our faces toward the settin' sun.

One by one the cares of life forever pass.

And we shall stand on the river bank at last.

CASEY

That's great! Hey why don't you let Jenny play it.

ERIC

How?

CASEY

Watch.

(CASEY helps JENNY up then sits down in the chair and takes her on his lap. JENNY acts like a young school- girl, loving the attention and giggling and being very coquettish. Then CASEY gets the guitar from ERIC who stands behind the chair and puts his arms around both of them and strums. They laugh as they sing:)

One by one the cares of life forever pass

And we shall stand upon the riverbank at last.

JENNY
Oh, you boys!

CASEY
That was great Jenny.
             (Helping her up and giving her back her chair.)

ERIC
Yeah, We'll have to do this again. Maybe I can teach you to play the guitar, Jenny.

CASEY
Right now we have to go get the Pizza.

             (EXIT CASEY yelling.)
Hey Ma, I need some cash.

ERIC
(To JENNY)
It's a beautiful song Jenny. It's kind of like a mantra. It lifts you out of one level and up on another, like climbing to the stars.
             (ERIC squeezes JENNY's hand. JENNY smiles and
             nods as if she understands.)

CASEY
Ready?

ERIC
Ready.

             (EXIT CASEY and ERIC)
             (Lights begin to dim, the rocking chair begins to rock
             and JENNY croons her song in an even younger voice.
             Her voice fades as the lights to down.)

We are going down the valley, one by one

With our faces toward the setting sun

One by one the cares of life forever pass

And we shall stand upon the riverbank at last.

(Lights dim to black.)

ACT II

Scene III

(Setting: Living room/kitchen setting.
At Rise: Time is the next day in the afternoon.BECKY seated on floor in living room folding newly washed clothes and putting clothes in basket.)

(ENTER BYRON)

BYRON

Doing your laundry too?

BECKY

Yeah, but I'm just about finished.

>(BYRON goes to refrigerator takes a drink of milk from the carton and returns it.)

Cathy doesn't have a washer and dryer?

BYRON

She used to go to the Laundromat before I moved in. Is that your laundry?

>(He scrutinizes the clothes in the basket.)

BECKY

What do you think? What do you think?

BYRON

I think you haven't got the balls to wear this.
(He holds up a jock strap.)

BECKY

(Laughing)
So, I'm doing John's too.
(Beat)
You like living with her?

BYRON

Cathy? Yeah. It's okay. She's very intelligent. She makes me think about things and we talk a lot. So, I'd say it was more positive than negative.

BECKY

Sounds like marriage.

BYRON

I guess it is.

(Buzzer from dryer sounds. BYRON walks out of room taking his box of clothes and brings back some of BECKY's clothes and dumps them in the basket.)

Do you feel any differently yet?

BECKY

Only hyper. I'm going bananas trying to stay off the grass. I haven't had any for almost 24 hours now. I can't think about this for seven months. I'll drive myself crazy.

BYRON

Weird, how things work.
                    (Wandering around kitchen.)

BECKY

Like what?

BYRON

Well, everything was just fine until Jenny came. Since then…

BECKY

Casey says she's just a little old lady and what's the big deal.

BYRON

I don't mean it negatively. I think she's part of our destiny. She's a motivator, a catalyst, to make us make changes and move along.

BECKY

Yeah, she does that all right. You look at her and realize we all have to die sometime, so we better get on with living.

BYRON

It's amazing to think that a person has the ability to influence lives even though they're old and out of their heads. Look what her presence has done since she's been here. You moved out and got pregnant, you're getting married, which you've always wanted to do. I think Lissa wanted to find some excuse to come home and touch base because the family means a lot to her. Casey, well, he's always been the most compassionate one of us but being the youngest, he never really expressed much.

BECKY

Yeah, this has been good for him because he always hides his feeling behind jokes and stuff. Now, he's not afraid to show them.

BYRON

Then there's Mom. She's like a different person, more her own person, since she got this job. She wouldn't have gone out to get it if she hadn't had Jenny to take care of. I know it looks like she's running away, but I think she's moving ahead in her own life.

BECKY

Yeah, but what about Dad?

BYRON

Dad. Well, Dad has always tried to work out problems logically and sometimes life isn't logical. I guess this whole thing has made him stop and review his own concepts. (Pause) I don't know what conclusions he's come to, if any, but it's jolted his thinking.

BECKY

And you?

BYRON

Well, I'm getting married too. I guess I'm no more sure that it will work out than you are. I guess I'm a lot like Dad, even though I don't want to be. I try to solve my problems in my head but it never gets transmitted to the rest of me. I never take action. This time, right or wrong, I will. All because we have an old lady in a rocking chair, waiting to die.

BECKY

You left out Austin.

BYRON

Austin? I usually do.
      (Ponders)
Well, I can't say he got caught because Jenny was here. I guess I don't have the answer. Maybe he has a secret death wish.

BECKY

Washer and dryer are all yours.

      (BYRON starts carrying his clothes to the laundry room.)

I figure we all die a little every day. Kind of growing toward death so that by the time it gets here it doesn't hurt so much.

BYRON

Funny, I look at it as if you're growing toward life, becoming free. You get rid of the body and mind and become spirit.

BECKY

But you believe in life after death or something, I don't.

BYRON

I believe in reincarnation. I see it in all living things. But I also think that there's death in living. When I first watched a snake lose its skin, I wondered if the snake thought it was going to die. The old skin had to die for the snake to get bigger. If that's the case, then life has death in it ... then, maybe death has life in it.

BECKY

Well, I could buy that. I just could never figure how when someone dies and goes back into the soil... how they ever evolve from dirt to a personality again.

BYRON

Cosmic copulation!

BECKY

Hey! Now that sounds interesting! (Laughing)

BYRON

Wanna try it with, say ... JOHN the Baptist or ... maybe St. JOHN?

BECKY

Oh sure, Mister Smartass!

(ENTER LISSA)

LISSA

You won't believe what happened. I went with Charlie and Jenny to the daycare center and then I hung around for awhile. The aide and I took Jenny out in the garden and the aide introduced her to another old lady in a wheel chair. The aid said she thought they would get along really well.

BECKY

So did they?

LISSA

Well, they just sat there. They didn't talk. Nothing. I tried to get them to talk.

BYRON

So you did all their talking for them.   (Teasingly)

LISSA

No.
                    (She playfully pushes him.)
But I did watch. I asked the other old lady her name. It was Joanne, or something like that. Then I asked her what she used to do. She turned around to Jenny and me and says, "I'm a registered nurse."

BECKY

Oh no! What did Jenny do?

LISSA

Jenny just looked at her like she didn't believe her.
                    (Pause)
She just turned her head away and kind of slumped down in her chair and never said another word.

BYRON

She stole Jenny's line.

LISSA

(Soberly)
It's worse than that I'm afraid. She stole her identity.

BECKY

What do you think that will do to Jenny?

LISSA

I don't know. She was really half dead before. That was her last vestige of self.

(EXIT BECKY to take her clothes out.)

BYRON

Well, I think … to Dad, Jenny's already dead. When he found out he couldn't make her rational, he just buried her. He forgot her, like she forgot him.

LISSA

Maybe not. Maybe she forgot someone who looks like him.

BYRON

What do you mean?

LISSA

I mean, Charlie doesn't look like her, so maybe he looks like his father, especially now that he's old and wrinkled. Maybe Jenny has blocked Dad out of her mind because he reminds her of the husband that abandoned her.

BYRON

Man, that's a different perspective, or should I say wrinkle.

LISSA

It's possible.

BYRON

A wrinkle (with humor), a wrinkle in time? Maybe death is only a wrinkle in time or a wrinkle in the nose of God, if he exists.

LISSA

HE? Why not SHE?

BYRON

Okay. Dad told me in the Christian Science Church when they say the Lord's Prayer, they say, Our Father, Mother, God. How about that? They were way ahead of women's rights.

LISSA

I didn't know it was such a progressive church. I wonder if they look kindly on lesbians.

(BECKY REENTERS with clothes.)

BECKY

Hey, I was gonna ask you about your friend … or partner. What's her name?

LISSA

Leslie.

BECKY

Leslie. Lissa and Leslie?

LISSA

Yes. We like alliteration … it sounds trippingly on the tongue.
			(She sticks her tongue out and wiggles it seductively.)

BECKY

Ooh God, Lissa. (with disgust) And you really love each other, and make love. I mean, I still…

LISSA

(Interrupts)

Look Becky, we've had this conversation over the phone dozens of times. If you want to know about Lesbian love, try it, don't knock it.

(EXIT LISSA)
BYRON

Dad also said, that instead of "Give us this day our daily bread", Christian Scientists say, "Give us grace for today, feed the famished affections."

BECKY

That's nice. What's that supposed to mean?

BYRON

It means all of us are hungry for love and none of us ever gets enough. Sometimes I think we equate love with getting attention, but attention span is short. Love is longer. Speaking of God and famished affections, how is Austin? And I'm hungry!

BECKY

He's out for a counseling session ... gone to a shrink. The attorney thought he'd have a better case if he had quote "sought counseling" and if you help me with the rest of these clothes, I'll make a sandwich for both of us.

(EXIT BYRON and BECKY. ENTER LISSA and KATE who is dressed in a pant suit with an armful of sheets.)

LISSA

... and you know, Mom, I'm sick of her snide inquiries into my love life. As if I couldn't get a man! I could and I wouldn't get a drug pusher. I just prefer women.

KATE

Oh Lissa,
(Putting her arm around her.)

don't make an issue of it. Who cares what Becky thinks. You lead your own life.

LISSA

Well, you understand, you never gave me a hard time. Why does she?

KATE

Lissa, I drink scotch now, all the time. But there was a time when the whole world was my cocktail. Your sister hasn't begun to live or face reality. Her world is very small.

LISSA

(Hesitantly)
What do you mean?
(Pause)
Did you have a homosexual experience?

KATE

Are you kidding? Working in New York? Working in Paris? Look Lissa, I love life ... ALL of it. (Beat) I figure most people have had some kind of homosexual experience or feelings.

LISSA

So you don't think you're born a homosexual?

KATE

Sex is sex, why label it? I just want my body to experience all the sensations it possibly can.

LISSA

So, how do you define homosexuality?

KATE

I don't. I think most people are AC/DC if they aren't inhibited. After all we have the same hormones. Who cares if some people are born homosexual or become homosexual because they've suffered some kind of abuse at the hands of the opposite sex. We're all looking for the same

thing, warmth, love, someone to cuddle with orgasms! I just think that everyone needs love at every age. I thought it was great that you wanted to find a girlfriend for Jenny.
(Laughs)

LISSA

Does Dad know?

KATE

Of course he knows. I used to take him to some of the gay bars and he loved it. As a matter of fact, I've often thought that if I hadn't come along in Charlie's life when I did, his innocence and naivete might have led him right into the gay world. He was very attractive and can be a bit effeminate, when he's insecure.

LISSA

Do you miss it. I mean, the other kind of relationship?

KATE

Sometimes.

LISSA

What about the others? Do they know?

KATE

I told Becky when I was trying to explain you to her. I'm sure she just turned it off. That's what Becky does if she doesn't want to hear something. As for the boys, no I haven't told them. (Pause) If you want to it's okay. I can handle it.

LISSA
(Pauses)
No, I kind of like sharing something with you. It's special.
(Beat)
If you liked it, why did you give it up?

KATE

I've always told you that making choices in life results in some kind of consequence. However, making choices also results in some kind of sacrifice. I wanted a home and family more than anything.

LISSA

Just like Becky.

KATE

Just like Becky.

LISSA

So that's why you understand her.
(Beat)
But you also understand me.

KATE

Yes, I do. Unlike Becky though, I really lived life to the hilt so that I knew what I was giving up to have a home and family. May I say, all of you were worth it.
(She hugs Lissa.)

(ENTER BYRON and BECKY with clothes.)

BYRON and BECKY
Wow! Get a load of you!

KATE

Yeah, Get a load. Have you gotten all your laundry done 'cause I
have a load of Jenny's sheets .
(Beat)
Think I look professional?

EVERYONE

Yeah!

BYRON

Let me help you.
(Byron takes the sheets from her.)
Becky's finished. I'm doing my wash now, but I only had one load.

KATE

Good. That gives me time to pour a drink. I could use one.

BECKY

I'll take one too, Mom.

LISSA

For someone who is so obsessed about having children, you sure don't seem to worry about what kind of nourishment they are getting as a fetus.

BECKY

(Becky stops pouring drink.)
Look Lissa, I'm having a hard enough time. I didn't know I was pregnant and I've been doing drugs ... and I'm terrified that something might be wrong.

LISSA

So, give it up.

BECKY

I'm trying to. I haven't done any heavy drugs since I found out, but giving up alcohol too, is a bit much to ask.

LISSA

Is it asking a bit much when your kid could be deformed and retarded or have other defects, just because their mother was too self-centered?

BECKY

Boy! I'd forgotten how much you like to preach. Okay, I won't drink, at least in front of you ... and I do worry, I'm very worried. I'm even having nightmares. Does that satisfy you?

KATE

Enough. Why can't the two of you grow up and learn to get along.
By the way, Lissa, I drank and smoked through all my pregnancies.
None of you came out with any noticeable defects … no fetal alcohol
syndrome.

LISSA

But Mom, they know more now.

KATE

Then how do they account for people like me? Of course, I didn't do
drugs.

LISSA

But alcohol is a drug.

KATE

Oh Lissa, you can't live someone else's life. You take your chances. I
guess my Irish luck held when it came to all of you. You know, I took
you to a psychiatrist because you were so hyperactive when you were a
kid and he prescribed valium for me. So, I guess I did my drugs after
the fact.

(ENTER CASEY and ERIC with basketball bouncing
it in kitchen. They go for beer.)

CASEY

Hey Kate, drinkin' again huh?
(Sipping his beer. KATE laughs and turns her back.)
So, what's new group?

BYRON

You're going to be the flower girl in Becky's wedding next weekend.

CASEY

No shit!
(Tossing ball back and forth to ERIC.)

I look really great in pink frilly dresses.

(He dances around.)

LISSA
And I get to be the best man ... how about that?

CASEY
Gee, Lissa, I never thought about that. You gonna wear a tux?

LISSA
Sure, you want me to? I look very good in a tux ... and a top hat too.
        (LISSA dances around like Fred Astaire and CASEY
        pinches her on the ass.)
Hey, Watch it!

CASEY
Dad's got the best job. He gets to give her away. Hey, the wedding
might be really good for Jenny too. Speaking of Jenny, where is she?

BECKY
Not home from the daycare center.

        (BECKY moves into the living room and the others
        follow. ERIC can't seem to get comfortable in the
        over-stuffed chair.)

CASEY
I wonder how she liked daycare.

LISSA
She didn't. Some other woman told Jenny that "she was a registered
nurse."

CASEY
I bet Jenny didn't like that. Somebody stole her line, huh?

ERIC

Didn't she even sing her song?

LISSA

Not that I know of.

ERIC

It's so soothing, like a lullaby. I just wonder where she learned it.

BECKY

Dad says it's something she learned when she was little.

(CASEY goes to kitchen for a beer.)

ERIC

Oh yeah, I also wanted to ask about Christian Science? What is it?

(CASEY walks in without a beer.)

CASEY

It's mind over matter. Like, if I were a Lowenbrau and I belonged to Austin, where in the refrigerator would I be hiding?
(Puts finger to forehead as if receiving a message.)
Ah ha, under the celery in the veggie bin.

(CASEY retreats to the kitchen again.)

BECKY

It's a Christian religion that believes you can heal yourself if you have enough faith and live a good life and read Mary Baker Eddy.

BYRON

It's more than mind over matter. It's the spirit of God. That's the crazy glue that binds mind and matter... but ya gotta have a healthy spirit for it to work.

ERIC

So, they don't believe in doctors, or take medicine, or drugs? Is it like alternative medicine?

BYRON

Something like that.

(ENTER CASEY with a Lowenbrau.)

CASEY

It's mind over matter, see, under the celery in the veggie bin. Want to split it with me Eric?
       (Handing it to Eric.)
Speaking of drugs, where's Austin?

BECKY

Austin's at the shrink's.

CASEY

No shit! Gee, I hope the guy can take it. The shrink, I mean.

BYRON

Dad and Jenny are here.

(ENTER CHARLIE and JENNY. CHARLIE helps her to the rocking chair. JENNY is noticeably weaker and more feeble – needs more help.)

CHARLIE

Hi. Say "Hi", Jenny. She isn't talking.

(JENNY doesn't even look up as CHARLIE speaks to her.)

KATE

Jenny, did you have a nice day?

(KATE walks over to JENNY. JENNY looks down into her lap.
KATE looks at CHARLIE who takes out a cigar, lights it, and walks away.)

Charlie.

(He turns around.)

Are you going to be ready to give your daughter away this weekend?

(KATE seats herself next to BYRON and BECKY on the couch.)

CHARLIE

My daughter?

(Absent minded.)

Oh, who?

(EVERYONE laughs.)

BYRON

Not Lissa, Dad.

LISSA

No, not me Dad.

CHARLIE

Oh, right. That leaves Becky. Right?

BECKY

Right, Dad.

(Disappointment in her voice.)

CHARLIE

Well, I've given away a few other things. but there's more joy attached to this. Just let me know what I'm supposed to do.

(CHARLIE goes to kitchen, pours a bourbon, walks through living room, pauses to look at his mother. Then EXITS.)

BECKY

Sure Dad.

LISSA

(To KATE)
Want me to help with dinner?

KATE

By God, there is some recompense in having children grow up.

(KATE gets up and LISSA joins her in the kitchen.
BYRON gets up walks around, CASEY tosses the ball
to ERIC who squirms in the chair.)

LISSA

Come on. Let's all go help. Come on Eric, you too. You're part of this
family and by your own choice yet. Are you sure it's better than being
at your own home?

ERIC

Oh yeah, a lot better. Believe me. My home is like the Roman
Coliseum. this place is like the Circus Maximus by comparison.

LISSA

I'm impressed, Casey has finally found a friend with some culture.

(ERIC rises slowly to follow LISSA.
BYRON sits down next to BECKY who hasn't made
a move.
CASEY is still bouncing the ball.
ERIC pats JENNY on the hand before he leaves.)

ERIC

Jenny, don't let that other woman bother you. Everyone here likes
you.

(EXIT ERIC)

BYRON

Oh hell, we might as well help too. Come on Casey. Coming Becky?

(EXIT BYRON and CASEY. BECKY moves over and sits by JENNY's chair. Lights dim and pinpoint light is on chair.)

BECKY

Come on Jenny. Don't stop talking now. I want you to talk to your great grandchildren. They can call you Grandma, can't they? Please talk.
(Beat)
I want somebody to tell me I'm doing the right thing.
(Almost in tears.)
I want somebody to give me their blessings, not just give me away.
(She sits back on her haunches.)

(JENNY lifts her arm as if it were very heavy and it lands, almost accidentally on BECKY's head, then slips off. BECKY gets up on her knees and tried to make eye contact with JENNY.)

Does that mean. it's okay? Is that a blessing?

KATE

Becky?

BECKY

I'm here. I'm coming.
(To JENNY)
Thanks Jenny. Maybe you do understand.

(EXIT BECKY leaving only Jenny in pinpoint lighting.
JENNY begins to sing her song in the voice of a young girl.)

JENNY

We are going down the valley, one by one

With our faces toward the setting sun

One by one the care of life forever pass

And we shall stand upon the riverbank at last.

(Lights to black.)

ACT II

Scene IV

(Setting: Living room/kitchen setting.
ERIC has taken his previous seat in the over-stuffed
chair and is squirming holding his Paper plate.
LISSA ENTERS and sits on sofa, with her plate,
followed by KATE and BECKY who find places to sit.
JENNY is in her chair, Not eating staring out at
audience.)

(AT Rise: The same day, a little later.)

BYRON

Austin's home.

(ENTER AUSTIN who walks over to the back of
JENNY's rocking chair, grabs it roughly – tipping it
back. He realizes what he's done. JENNY is startled.
Then AUSTIN heads to the refrigerator for a beer.)

CASEY
(CASEY is still in the kitchen getting himself a beer
and one for ERIC. As he moves toward the living
room he says:)

Does the world look any different from a horizontal position?
(Handing a beer to ERIC.)

AUSTIN
(To KATE)
What's he talking about?

KATE

Ask him.

CASEY
Don't you lie down for a shrink?

AUSTIN
Not me.I'm too hyper. I'm going crazy. I've been off everything for 32 hours and I'm not gonna make it. I can't quit cold turkey.

(AUSTIN demonstrates hyperactivity. He picks up dishes, slams them down he knocks cockroaches off the kitchen counter. He stamps then on the floor.)

God! I wish these were real roaches, the other kind. I hate shrinks.

CHARLIE
You can make it, Austin. Just put your mind to it. You know your mind can fantasize much better than any drug.

(CHARLIE pours a drink.)

KATE
Charlie, you don't know what you're talking about. Leave him alone.

AUSTIN
It's my fucking body… it wants…and it wants.
(Beat)
I had a seizure in the shrink's office.
(Silence)
Yeah, I guess I was horizontal. One minute I was up; the next minute I was on the floor.   I don't know how long it was, but man, I couldn't remember where I was. My body ached.
(Pause)

I had one once before. It was the drugs.

>(AUSTIN looks to KATE for compassion and KATE comes over to him and sits down next to him.)

BYRON

Did you think you had died?

AUSTIN

That's what it felt like.

CHARLIE

We'll need to figure out what will counteract those things.

BECKY

How do you feel now?
>(Going over to AUSTIN and patting him on the back.)

AUSTIN

Like hell.

LISSA

>(Grabs AUSTIN's arm, pulls him off balance and gets him on the floor. Then she sits on top of him.)

You listen to me Austin, you sit and cry "poor me" when it's something of your own doing. You make me sick. I deal with kids everyday who have seizures, who can't see, who can't hear, who can't move, and it's not their fault. Those (she gets teary) kids try. It takes every ounce of their little strength to push a button or key on a computer and for what, to someday be able to hold some small job that would put them in the mainstream of society hoping to appear normal, hoping people won't think they're queer, abnormal. I wish I had half the courage my kids have. That's why people like you make me so angry. You sit there and cry the blues when you have everything at your fingertips to make your life different.

(LISSA gets up.)

Why in the hell don't you get up off your fat ass and do something for yourself? I have no sympathy for you.

AUSTIN

(Slowly getting up.)

You bitch!

LISSA

You're right. I am. But if I were in your shoes, I would have the guts to do something. They have a lot of good drug rehab programs. Why don't you check into one. It might also be smart if we checked on counseling for dysfunctional families.

BECKY

Dysfunctional?

BYRON

WE are not a dysfunctional family. One of my psychologists suggested I was the product of a dysfunctional family, and I came home and told Dad. He promptly informed me the guy didn't know what he was talking about. Right Dad?

CHARLIE

That's correct. These people label others without knowing the English language. Dis-functional means that you don't function. This family functions. Now if he wanted to imply we don't function as everyone else functions, then he should have said we were A-functional, away from the norm, which in today's society I don't see as a major detriment.

CASEY

Aw come on, I'm so bored with all this heavy shit.

(In a New York accent.)

Dis-function.

We are gonna have dis function called a wedding in just a few days. Dis function al be held in dis joint, to dis-perse any illegalities about Becky's baby. Dis-function al dis- turb the neighbors and give everyone a chance to get dis-gustingly drunk. Now, that's something to look forward to.

ERIC

Hey Casey, I think I'd better dis-appear. Okay?

CASEY

Hey man, you don't have to go. This kind of stuff is normal around here. This is where abnormal is normal.

ERIC
(ERIC picks up the basketball which is near his chair, rolls it in the direction of JENNY's chair.)

Yeah, well I gotta few things I gotta do and then I gotta go to work.

(As ERIC stands up his hands slip down by the side of the cushion.)

JESUS! What in the hell.

CASEY

God, what's the matter?

(CASEY goes over to look as do the others. CASEY laughs.)

Hey, look what Eric found. Leonardo. How's it feel to sit on a boa constrictor, Eric?

ERIC
Shit! I don't know. I don't know. Scary!

LISSA

God! Byron, you still have that stupid boa?

BYRON

I'll take him. God he must be starved! But he's alive! I was afraid I had lost him for good. Thanks for finding him for me.   He won't hurt you and Eric knows that, and he's not stupid. Leonardo is very friendly.

ERIC
(ERIC pats the boa.)
Well, I'm glad he didn't bite me.

CASEY

Boas don't bite; they put the squeeze on you.

BYRON

They go for weeks without getting really hungry enough to bite. Hey Eric, before you go, how about holding the cage door open for me while I get him in the cage. I sometimes forget to lock it 'cause I hate to put living things in a cage.

ERIC

Sure. I just have to hold the door, right?

(BYRON and ERIC EXIT with Leonardo.)

LISSA
(Yelling)
Hey Eric… remember, circuses come with wild animal acts.

BECKY

Poor guy. This family must overwhelm him.

KATE

Why, we're perfectly normal.

(CASEY goes over to JENNY's chair to retrieve the ball. JENNY has slipped down in her chair, her eyes are partly open as is her mouth.)

AUSTIN

Yeah normal.

CASEY
(CASEY picks up ball and looks at JENNY.)

Jenny.

(He touches her hand.)

Jenny. Jenny,

(He sits on the floor with the ball in his hands and stares at the group.)

(KATE walks over to JENNY. She feels her face, touches her hand and then closes her eyes.)

KATE

Charlie.

(She nods "Yes" to him.)

(CHARLIE looks at KATE.
BECKY goes over to join KATE.)

BECKY

She's not... she's... dead?

(BYRON and ERIC REENTER. They realize what has happened and move over to JENNY's chair. ERIC finds his guitar. Austin joins them.)

AUSTIN

Oh, God, she is.

(AUSTIN touches the rocking chair and EXITS
ERIC begins to strum his guitar quietly, playing JENNY's song.
KATE turns and walks over to CHARLIE. She puts her arm around him and the two of them EXIT slowly.

BECKY touches JENNY's hand and cries softly as she
EXITS behind KATE and CHARLIE.)

BYRON

Oh no.
　　　(He has a hard time swallowing.)
Well Jenny, at least you're free.

(LISSA puts her arm around BYRON.)

LISSA
(To JENNY)
You won't need a girl friend now… and Jenny, you can be a registered
nurse again.

(ERIC's guitar music fades as he EXITS with BYRON
and LISSA.)

CASEY

I knew it would happen right here. I knew it. I just knew it.

(CASEY puts his head down on the ball and cries.)

(REENTER CHARLIE who helps CASEY up from
the floor.
CASEY rises slowly and EXITS bouncing the ball as
he goes.)

CHARLIE
(Looking at his mother.)
Only when you drink from the river of silence shall you sing.

(CHARLIE turns his back and as he EXITS, he sings
JENNY's song.)

We are going down the valley one by one

With our faces toward the setting sun

One by one the cares of life forever pass

And we shall stand upon the riverbank at last.

(The lights have been dimming as each group left the stage until after CASEY has left there is only a pinpoint light left on JENNY and then it too dims to black.)

(EXIT JENNY)

Curtain Call: Lights come up from black slightly to show ERIC enter stage right with his guitar. He takes a few steps and looks over at JENNY's empty chair. He moves back a few steps and sits on stage and begins to strum the song.

LISSA follows ERIC and sits next to him. Lights come up further to reveal five additional rocking chairs.

CASEY comes in and sits in one, with the ball in hand.

BECKY enters and sits next to CASEY in rocking chair, she rubs her belly like a pregnant woman does.

BYRON comes in next and takes a lotus position in his rocker. AUSTIN comes in next and sits on the floor, looks over at JENNY's chair and body rocks with his head in his hands.

CHARLIE enters with drink and sits in his rocker and just stares at audience.

KATE enters with a drink in her hand and sprawls in her rocker. Finally JENNY enters and sits in her chair.

Cast rises together and take bows.

(Lights dim to black.)

NOTES

KATE and CHARLIE are never without a drink or getting a drink.

CHARLIE smokes cigars. KATE cigarettes.

AUSTIN, CASEY, BECKY and BYRON are all body rockers so throughout the play they may body rock.

A great deal of physical humor can be added by the actors-body language indicative of drinking, drugs, pregnancy, etc.

COSTUMES

ACT I:

CHARLIE – overcoat and suit

Later short shorts

Colorful boxers

KATE – shorts and T-shirts

JENNY – several layers of clothes

Dress – two sweaters and a coat and hat.

AUSTIN – sports jacket and slacks

Others – shorts – jeans – and T-shirts.

ACT II

CHARLIE – slacks and polo shirt

KATE – pant suit

JENNY – dress with sweater

AUSTIN – slacks and sport shirt

LISSA – suit or pant suit

Others – shorts, jean, and T-shirts

PROPERTIES

Boa Constrictor

Booze bottles

Brief case

Brownie mix

Furniture

Guitar

Jock strap

KATE's sipper

Kitchen Facilities

Laundry

Mixing bowl

Pizza

Rolled reefers

Round table

Soup bowl

Stash baggie

Tea cups